Quick Fix

The small changes that make a big difference

Quick Fix
Your Web Life

Bruce Durie

How To Books

Published by How To Books Ltd,
3 Newtec Place, Magdalen Road,
Oxford OX4 1RE, United Kingdom.
Tel: (01865) 793806. Fax: (01865) 248780.
email: info@howtobooks.co.uk
http://www.howtobooks.co.uk

British Library Cataloguing in Publication Data.

A catalogue record for this book is available from the British
Library.

Cover design by Shireen Nathoo Design, London
Cover illustration by Roger Langridge
Cartoons by Grizelda Grizlingham

Produced for How To Books by Deer Park Productions
Designed and Typeset by Shireen Nathoo Design, London
Printed and bound in Great Britain by The Baskerville Press Ltd.
Salisbury, Wiltshire

NOTE: The material contained in this book is set out in good faith
for general guidance and no liability can be accepted for loss or
expense incurred as a result of relying in particular circumstances
on statements made in the book. Laws and regulations are
complex and liable to change, and readers should check the
current position with the relevant authorities before making
personal arrangements.

Contents

About the Author

Bruce Durie divides his time between writing and consultancy. He is the author of *Creating a Web Site*, *1000 Best Web Sites* and *e-Business* for How To Books as well as other non-fiction, novels, video scripts, poetry and plays. He constructs web sites, both for commercial clients and for his own amusement. Previously Director of the Edinburgh International Science Festival and a senior figure at various universities, he lives in Fife, Scotland, with his young son.

Introduction

This book is intended to be a collection of those tips, tricks and web sites which have made one person's online life happier and less infuriating. They are presented here in the hope that others' online lives will be made that little bit better for knowing them. Then you can get on with the business of driving your PC rather than trying to jump-start it on cold mornings.

Computers should also be fun. There is very little point in using them if they add to your store of troubles rather than decrease them, and there is no point at all in using them if they aggravate more than they help. So you have to know enough about them to get the best from them.

Most pages have a Tip which will help you get around some of the more frustrating aspects of computers. However, they are not just about troubleshooting – some of them may address an issue you didn't know you had or help you achieve something you hadn't realised was possible. A number of them are "professional secrets" rarely documented elsewhere. You may choose to go through them sequentially or dip into them when you have a particular problem.

The book also has carefully-selected web sites as jumping-off places for exploring the world wide web. The web sites are arranged into categories, for ease of reference and are listed on the following pages. In some cases it was a judgement call whether a site went into one category or another – are Museums sites to do with Education or Reference, for instance? The list will be a help in case of confusion.

These sites were chosen as good general introductions to a particular area of the web, and in many cases contain links to other, relevant sites. Explore them at your leisure. Many will be useful for school and work projects. You can use this book as you wish, take it a page at a time or keep it as a reference. It's your online life – live it to the full!

Note for younger readers:
Just as there are video recorders so complicated that only an eight-year-old can program them, computers seem to work better in the hands of younger people. Be gentle with the adults around you – they were probably born before anyone walked on the moon and in some cases when dinosaurs roamed the earth. Most of them are frightened witless of the computer and will need your patient, careful guidance.

Bruce Durie

This book is dedicated to Jamie
and to everyone else who has asked:
"How do I make my computer behave?"

List of Tips

Modem and comms tips

Newsgroups

Speed-up tips

Windows tips

List of Sites

Fun Learning

Holidays and Travel

Managing Your Money

Non-Stop Shopping

Only On the web

List of Sites

More tips and web site updates at:

http://www.fifeweb.net/qfywl/

Notify changed or broken links to:

qfywl@fifeweb.net

Chapter 1

Food and Wine

Books-For-Cooks

COOKERY

http://www.Books-for-Cooks.com/

Want a cookbook? This is the place – a specialist bookstore-cum-website. Even if you never buy a book there is an immense amount of information for food lovers here, including recipes. Very American, but that in itself means a diversity of ethnic cookery information.

The Cyberspace Wine Map

WINE

http://www.winebiz.com/

This is a trade site about wine, originating in Napa Valley, California, home of what Americans call domestic wines. It is a treasure chest of information about wines and their enjoyment. Pour a glass and dip in.

Speed-up tip

Turn off Windows animation – When you Minimise or Restore a window, it animates. This is pretty but takes up time and resources. It can be turned off by altering the Registry settings. Close any open programs, click Start, Run, type regedit, click OK, click on HKEY_CURRENT_USER and keep expanding the + signs until you get to Control Panel, Desktop, WindowMetrics. Click on this, right-click on any empty space in the right pane and select New/String Value, click on the new item which appears at the bottom of the list, type in MinAnimate, right-click on this, click Modify and enter a value of 0 for off or 1 for on. Close regedit.exe then shut down and restart the computer.

Dad's in the Kitchen   COOKERY

http://www.dinersgrapevine.com/dik/index.html

Oh, yes! A web site dedicated to the idea that fathers can cook too, if they only but tried. Nice idea, funny graphics and tidy execution.

Euromenu

COOKERY

http://www.euromenu.com/

This site provides a search of restaurants in France,
Spain, Italy, Ireland, Scotland, England and Wales
by a long list of cuisine types – including, helpfully,
non-smoking and Family Pub. It is simple, effective
and well-designed and helps narrow down the
search for a good night out. There is no Cajun in
Cardiff but there is a Brasserie in Belfast. The nice
touch is that it displays the menu.

The Global Gastronomer

COOKERY

http://www.cs.yale.edu/~hupfer/global/gastronomer.html

Select a region from the
clickable map and escuriate
your way through the
world's cooking. A great
site, nicely executed and
fun. Foods of Antarctica
deserves a special
mention.

Start-up tip

Desktop shortcuts on the toolbar – Right-click in the Windows 98 quick launch toolbar (bottom right, next to start) select Toolbars, Desktop. All your Desktop shortcuts are now on the toolbar and are accessible without clicking Minimise All.

Interactive Food Finder

DINING

http://www.olen.com/food/

Would you like to know the nutritional information for more than 1,000 items in a fast-food restaurant? Search here by calories, fat, cholesterol and sodium. Clearly the Minnesota Attorney General's Office, on whose work this site is based, is a true, if unlikely, subversive. A fun idea, with a useful, healthy purpose. If I mentioned the take-away chain with the highest percentage of fat in the burgers, I would be sued. You can check for yourself.

Kids & Co.   COOKERY

http://www.intelligent-era.co.uk/kids%26co/

Worried about what the kids eat and whether all the
junkfood is damaging? This UK childcare site is for
anyone who is involved in looking after children, or
looking for childcare. It contains useful information
on children's nutrition and foods which justifies its
inclusion here. There are suggested dishes for
toddlers and fun recipes for children to make plus
creative ideas for things to make. A caring site.

Mimi's Cyber Kitchen   COOKERY

http://www.cyber-kitchen.com/

This may well be the largest and most complete
food and cookery site on the web. There are links to
hundreds of other food-related sites, plus recipes.

Start-up tip

Password length – Force a minimum password length – Start, Run, type regedit. exe, click OK and go to HKLM\SOFTWARE\Microsoft \Windows\CurrentVersion\ Policies\Network. Edit, New, Binary value, call it MinPwdLen and give it a number as your minimum length.

SOAR   COOKERY

http://soar.berkeley.edu/recipes/

Need the correct recipe for Gesztenye Kremlèves (cream of chestnut soup) but can't lay your hands on it? Start with SOAR (The Searchable Online Archive of Recipes) and find anything you want. The site is also indexed by major eating opportunities (breakfasts, appetisers, Christmas, etc.) and by ethnic groups. A great resource for the kitchen wizard.

Wine & Dine e-Zine   WINE

http://www.winedine.co.uk/

This is a delightful site – idiosyncratic, opinionated, quirky and guaranteed to appeal to the guzzler in us all. It also has some amazing things for sale that say a lot about the web author, Tony le Ray (a cure for snoring, for one).

Wine & Dine Restaurants   DINING

http://www.winedine.co.uk/thedines.html

I seriously doubt that there is a more comprehensive or worthwhile guide to restaurants anywhere on the web. It is not extensive, but each eaterie is rolled around in the mouth and savoured by seasoned wine and food writers. The site is spoilt by poor execution and looks like somebody finished off the HTML code after a rather good lunch. However, it's one to write on the back of a menu and take home.

Wine Links   WINE

`http://www.speakeasy.org/~winepage/winelink.html`

This is a site of links to other web sites about wine.
Much of the web consists of nothing more than
pointers to other sites. However, this site offers
context as well, with a commentary on each site
chosen. Someone has done a great deal of
homework here, so profit from it.

The Wine Page   WINE

`http://www.speakeasy.org/~winepage/`

This is a real hidden site – nobody knows it exists
and there's no way to get there from the
www.speakeasy.org main site that I can see. But it is
just packed with wine information. A full-bodied
subsite with a lingering afterglow. In particular, look
at **http://www.speakeasy.org/~winepage/cellar/codedfaq.
html#9**

Chapter Two

Holidays and Travel

All Countries Of The World   TRAVEL

http://www.inweh.unu.edu/unuinweh/mappage.htm

This is just what it says – links to each country,
organised by the United Nations University in
Tokyo. But it is fairly unselective and some of the
targets are of poor quality or not quite the best.
Why would they have chosen **http://www.britain.co.uk/**,
which is very good but hardly official, over the UK
government site of the Tourist Board? Still, if you
need to find out quickly about where they mine
phosphates in Nuaru, do start here.

Web tip

Find a good portal and stick with it – Portals are Web pages with, in theory, everything on them that you would need – navigation, new, TV listings, searches – and act as a place to start your Web surfing. They take the guesswork out of finding the right place to go first. I humbly suggest http://www.fifeweb.net/

Auto Europe

TRAVEL

http://www.autoeurope.com/

Want to hire a car anywhere in Europe? Then find hotels and travel information for your visits along the way? Auto Europe has a straightforward booking and enquiry form, with no need to give credit card details until actually making a reservation and no cancellation fees. This is a very useful site for the foot-loose traveller.

Britannia   TRAVEL

http://britannia.com/

This is an absolutely huge site, encyclopaedic in its
scope, containing everything about Britain.
Constructed in the USA and registered in Delaware
(which is probably a tax dodge), the site has mostly
UK contributers and is a superb place to start for
anyone interested in Britain, its history, institutions,
tourist attractions and lots more. Despite the US
origins, it is supremely useful for Brits too.

Bus and Coach UK   TRAVEL

http://nationalexpress.co.uk/

This site goes one further than Railtrack's (page 43)
by taking all the necessary details then allowing
online booking. There are also special offers, day
trips and discount schemes. A simple, effective
site that delivers exactly what
you expect.

Web tip

Web rings – Web sites can be organised into loose confederations of like-minded or similar-subject Web rings which may also include advertisers. Their great merit is that they cut down browsing time – anyone into Tolkein will probably join The One Ring (yes, it's really called that) and if your site is relevant enough to get included, they may visit you, too. To find a ring, type Webring and your chosen subject in your search engine.

Cheap Flights   TRAVEL

http://www.cheapflights.co.uk/

This may well be the best source for travel bargains from the UK, and you don't even have to register. It takes you to a selection of agents with flights to the places you indicate, which saves searching the pages of other agents and airlines. Special deals, last minute bookings plus car and hotel reservation are available – a gem of a site and easy to use.

City.Net   TRAVEL

http://www.city.net/

This is Excite's travel search engine and it has a
wealth of information beyond basic destination
information, including a Find the Lowest Fare
facility that only works for US cities of departure.
Shame really.

Complete Skier   TRAVEL

http://www.complete-skier.com/

In 1998 I counted 48 ski sites and 150 in November
1999. Fortunately, the choice of the best one or two
was easy because most are as useless as concrete
snow boots. Complete Skier has the usual resort
guides, snow reports, technique tips and pre-ski
exercises, but also boasts a chalet-booking service.
And it looks good, as must we all while tumbling
uncontrollably downhill.

Web tip

Measuring site speed – Site speed is the time (in seconds) needed for a user to download and view your start page at 28.8Kbps using a dial-up connection. Many people use 56K modems, ISDN or leased lines, but a lot don't. So design your site for the lowest common denominator. Any more than ten seconds and you'll lose them. If your page is slow to download, cut down the graphics, clever Java and dynamic HTML effects, or use a gif or jpg optimiser to compress your graphics and reduce download time. Does your gif logo need to be in 16 million colours when 16 might do? So after you have uploaded your site, open it in your browser, click Refresh or Reload and time it.

Disney Theme Park and Resort Sites TRAVEL

http://www.mcs.net/~werner/links.html

This unofficial Disney Parks site contains all the links to all Disney sites, official or otherwise. It's a lot of information in one place and a good place to begin any exploration of the world of Walt.

Euro Metro   TRAVEL

http://www.metropla.net

This is a truly useful site, albeit specialised – maps
of every underground, metro and subway system. It
is fronted up by a clickable map of the world.
Within each city's metro map is information about
the place itself and other useful links. Definitely
worth a look.

Expedia   TRAVEL

http://www.expedia.co.uk/

I hate to admit it, but this Microsoft site probably
deserves to be the world's busiest travel web.
Simultaneous searches of full and discount
scheduled air fares throw up great bargains on
occasion and the booking
time is scorching hot
compared with some of the
clunky versions around.

Web tip

Design tip – image maps –
An image map is a picture
in a web page which
contains a number of links
at different places within
the image. Clicking on each
'hot spot' links to a different
file. This is fine and can be
extremely effective –
imagine a map of Europe
where clicking on each
country took you to the
page describing the wine of
that country, say. But, if the
web browser has the
graphics turned off, it won't
work. So always provide
textual hyperlinks as well.

Fodor's Travel Online   TRAVEL

http://www.fodors.com

Fodor's Guides have a justified reputation for being
detailed and useful. If anything, the web site is even
more so. Apart from the expected features there is a
facility to generate an itinerary based on
destination, chosen price range, travel plans, etc. It
then gives you what is basically a battle plan for
your holiday. Impressive!

Foreign Languages   TRAVEL ADVICE

http://http://www.travlang.com/languages/

This site in 70 languages offers language learning, a
free email Word of the Day service, translation of a
particular word or phrase, translating dictionaries
and a free downloadable multi-lingual dictionary
program for Windows, called Ergane.

Health Advice for Travellers   TRAVEL ADVICE

http://www.doh.gov.uk/hat/emerg.htm

This is another official government site, and a good
one at that. Where else could you find out whether
your trip to Ougadougou will require vaccinations
for dengue, Rocky Mountain spotted fever or
cholera, and which malaria tablets to take to which
country? There is also a wealth of local information
that will be useful to anyone planning a trip to out
of the way places. Excellent, straightforward site.

Web tip

Searching for software –
You can spend hours in
search engines finding the
best software for a
particular job. Or you may
not even know that a
particular piece of software
exists, or even that you
need it. Software archives
with links to downloads are
the answer. Good examples
are download.com and
softspeak.com.

How Far Is It?   TRAVEL ADVICE

http://www.indo.com/distance/

This is a great idea – select your starting point and
destination and get the distance, plus a map from
the Xerox Palo Alto Research Center. Then zoom in
to see more and more detail. Simple and useful.

Leisureplan   TRAVEL ADVICE

http://www.leisureplan.com

View colour photos of over 13,000 hotels before
you make a reservation. Links allow you to search
for the lowest plane fares, rent a car, book transport
at your destination, plan a cruise, get hints and

detailed destination descriptions, plan a trip, then book everything online – easy!

Mapquest
TRAVEL ADVICE

http://www.mapquest.com/

Almost every major city in the world – and a few of the smaller ones – are in MapQuest's database. The level of detail ranges from large-scale plans showing major routes in and out to individual streets, with locations of important facilities (hotels, theatres, banks, etc.) shown. There are also links to other resources – weather, restaurants, accommodation, local information and so forth. The maps can be printed and come out best on a decent colour printer.

Multi Media Mapping
TRAVEL ADVICE

http://uk.multimap.com/howto.htm

This is a wonderful idea – UK maps within your web pages. Provide surfers with a map showing the places described on your pages or include a small map in your page, showing the places the page relates to, suh as your address or general area. The only information needed is the full postcode embedded in a link. This is a free service, but larger maps, individual support, etc. are available for a fee.

Net Café Guide   TRAVEL ADVICE

http://www.netcafeguide.com/

I once met a man having serious withdrawal symptoms because he couldn't access his email on a Greek island. I thought that was largely the point of going there, but I told him the URL of this guide to more than 2,400 cybercafés in 120 countries and he was 100 yards down the beach before he realised he didn't know where to go to access a computer, which is where we came in. How we laughed!

RAC   TRAVEL ADVICE

http://rac.co.uk/

Anyone planning a road trip should access route planning and then traffic news. The print-out of route, distance, times and traffic alerts will speed your journey no end. The main part of the site –

called Digital Services – is an excellent example of complicated information handled simply and well.

Railtrack   TRAVEL ADVICE

http://www.railtrack.co.uk/

This is exactly what the web is best at – making sense of complex information stored on a database and presenting it simply. No more long calls to busy and uninformed booking agents – just work out where you start from, where you finish, whether you want to go direct or the pretty way and your departure or arrival time and the site will show you the best trains around the indicated times. There is no facility to book tickets, but print out a copy of the schedule and take it to the station – it should cut your booking time in half at least.

Roadside America   TRAVEL ADVICE

http://www.roadsideamerica.com/

Next time I go across the USA I will definitely print off every place on my route from this site. Over 6,000 offbeat visitor attractions figure, from the

fabled urinating ox statue in Montana to the
Washington Apple Maggot Quarantine Area by way
of the Church of Elvis in Oregon. Good listings of
children's attractions feature. It's like having
Garrison Keillor, Will Rogers and Bill Bryson all in
the back of the car.

Rough Guide   TRAVEL ADVICE

http://www.roughguides.com/

Like Fodor's and Berlitz, Rough Guides are well
known in their print format. The web guide is
amazing. There are more than 3,500 places on the
database and an excellent search engine to reach
them. A related e-zine site has more in-depth
articles on many of these and there are excellent
tips for the traveller and visitor. An email newsletter
(free) will keep you updated. Good visuals.

Terraserver   TRAVEL ADVICE

http://www.terraserver.com/

Oh yes! Images from Rusian spy satellites. Type in
your location or click on a map and home in on

your home. Or anyone else's. Good images of natural resources (Niagara Falls, volcanoes), well-known buildings and whole cities. This is better than any map.

Tourism Offices Worldwide   TRAVEL ADVICE

http://www.towd.com/

This is another one of those obvious but great ideas – a listing of tourist offices by destination and – extremely useful – where to find one country's offices in another country. There are also links to country and destination web sites and other contact information (phone, fax, etc.). In combination with the Rough Guide (above) it makes planning a trip a pleasure instead of a logistical nightmare. What makes the web site itself attractive is the lack of advertising and annoying banners and pop-ups.

Travel Resources   TRAVEL ADVICE

http://www.travel-resources.com/

Not every guide book can tell you everything. Sometimes the best tips come from others who have travelled before. And that's what this site is – a grab-bag of useful and relevant information about a country, city or region with links others have discovered that will be useful. Pay back the compliment – leave your own favourite links on the site and keep it growing.

Chapter Three

Career Choices

The Careers Gateway

http://www.careersoft.co.uk/

Nicely designed and fast, this comprehensive web site is aimed at UK careers, education and guidance specialists and teachers. There are also links to the web sites of professional bodies, universities and other resources to help with job finding, plus a range of useful teaching ideas and resources.

Speed-up tip

Set the Task Scheduler –
Run your maintenance
tasks regularly. Run them
every night (for heavy
users) or once a week, with
a one hour interval
between each task, in this
order – Cleanup; ScanDisk;
Disk Defragment. Set
ScanDisk to automatically
fix errors.

Career Opportunities in the UK

http://www.topjobs.co.uk/hayward/haywarda.htm

This well-designed, fast and exceptionally well-
thought-out site can access information on a wide
variety of career opportunities in the UK. Register a
job category and region of work and be notified by
email when a job matching your search criteria
arises. There are also links to information about the
geographic area selected for job search, a useful
feature if thinking of relocation.

Gisajob

http://www.gisajob.co.uk/

One of those domain names you wish you'd thought of yourself, Gisajob claims to have 85,000 jobs at any one time, with almost 3,000 registered agencies.

Gradunet–Virtual Careers Office

http://www.gradunet.co.uk/Scripts/WebObjects.exe/Gradu net.woa

This Virtual Careers Office is a very cutely implemented job hunt site – and more. Good extra features include a searchable careers events list and a facility to log your spoken and written fluency in a variety of foreign languages. The geographic index is a great help and there are listings of voluntary sector jobs.

Speed-up tip

Registry backup – You can take a backup copy of your Registry settings (in fact, you can take up to nine!) by using D:/other/misc/cfgback/cfgback.exe on your Windows CD. Alternatively, use Start, Run, type regedit, click OK then click Registry Export Registry File to save in .reg format. This stores files in *.rbk format. This is useful before major upgrades, big installations, etc.

Jig-Cal Careers Research Centre

http://www.jig.ed.ac.uk/

The University of Edinburgh provides a range of careers-related software, resources, information, advice and guidance. More aimed at careers specialists and advisers, it has a wealth of useful information for job-hunters.

Jobcenter

http://www.jobcenter.com/

Excellent, attractive design marks this site out as
something special. It also has online interviewing
by videolink. You may not want to apply for any of
the US hi-tech jobs on offer, but for anyone in the
careers business, or considering recruitment online,
look here to see how it should be done.

Milkround Online

http://www.milkround.co.uk/

The Milkround was originally meant as a put-down
for the annual trek of employers around the
universities, trawling for graduates. Now it is the
official title for this well-respected activity and even
has its own web site. Apart from the usual job
search and company profiling facilities, it has a
useful Careers Advice section dealing with CVs,
covering letters, interview skills, assessment centres,
temping and other topics.

Monster.Com

http://www.occ.com/

Although this is an American site, it does have
international reach with job opportunities far and
wide, including the UK. There are claimed to be
almost 200,000 job opportunities and millions of
job prospects on the database. A Job Search Agent
allows you to find jobs and apply for them. There is
also a CV Builder to help with applications.

Prospects Web

http://www.prospects.csu.man.ac.uk/

This is the essential guide to graduate jobs,
postgraduate courses and careers information in the
UK and enables students, graduates and employers
to connect directly to an up-to-date online job
match and email recruitment service. There are also
career guides and profiles for different types of
work, as well as computerised careers guidance
software. Authoritative, complete and containing
the latest information, it is an excellent web
implementation of an excellent service.

The Recruitment Database

http://www.enterprise.net/recruitmentdb/

Say you are an engineer, looking for a post in the petroleum industry in the Midlands. You could post your CV on a database that employers can search. This site provides the software (free) which allows you to upload your CV, but also has a vacancies listing and a separate area for employers, agencies, head-hunters and consultants (paid for). Database recruiting is an increasing trend and this is a good example of how it works.

Supermodel

http://www.supermodel.com/

Couldn't resist it – one for the Wannabes.
Everything you need to know about starting out as a
professional model. They're all here: Cindy
Crawford, Claudia Schiffer, Naomi Campbell, Kate
Moss. You can also purchase your own official
Supermodel merchandise – posters, calendars,
videos and t-shirts – and get news, gossip and so
forth. Dream on!

University of London Careers Service

http://www.careers.lon.ac.uk/

Don't be put off by the title – you may not be a
student or graduate of London but this excellent
site can offer help on careers-related topics,
choosing a job, CVs and interviews. There is also a
Careers Events listing, regularly updated part-time,
temporary, voluntary and vacation jobs, a Virtual
Careers Library and a growing categorised list of
links to online careers resources. Superb!

Chapter Four

Fitness and Health

Aidsmap

http://www.aidsmap.com/

Anyone who is confused about HIV and AIDS, prevention, treatment and myth-busting, should begin with this site from a consortium of official and semi-official bodies. The design is taken from the London Underground map and makes for easy navigation through a mass of complex but plain-language detail. This is a good example of a site where as much thought has gone into how to make information readily available as into the information itself, which is a welcome rarity.

Speed-up tip

System Monitor – If your system seems slow and unresponsive, use System Monitor to pin down the culprit. System Monitor is on the Win 95 CD, but does not install in the Typical option – use Custom, Start, Programs, Accessories, System Tools, System Monitor or Start, Run and type sysmon. Monitor Kernel Processor Usage – with no programs running, this should be near zero. Click View, Always on top and check the SysMon screen as you work.

The Alternative Guide

http://www.altguide.com

This is the online version of the *Alternative Guide to Complementary Health and Healing in London and the South of England* seen in healthfood shops and other stores. Although biased to the London area, it has generally useful information on everything from Acupuncture to Zone Therapy (taking in Laughter Therapy on the way).

The Body Shop

http://www.thebodyshop.co.uk/

Campaigning is their business as much as selling skin and hair care. So salve your conscience with their salves and become an interactivist while you tittivate.

Center for Disease Control and Prevention

http://www.cdc.gov/

The CDC is America's (and to some extent the world's) watchdog on disease, their spread and their control. The best feature of the site is its extremely comprehensive searchable database which produces technical and up-to-date references (some in Adobe Acrobat pdf format) on almost any disease. The Travellers Health tips are also extremely good if somewhat alarmist in a well-meaning way.

Speed-up tip

Swap file and virtual memory – This is an area of your hard drive set aside to simulate your PC's memory and should be optimised – not too big and not too small – to minimise the amount of resizing, hard drive 'thrashing' and other unwelcome events.

Windows will calculate the right size for you. Right-click My Computer, Properties, General and note how much memory (RAM) you have. Click on Performance, Virtual Memory. It's usually best to let Windows manage your Virtual Memory settings.

Dr Lockie

http://www.drlockie.com/

The good doctor is a leading homeopathic practitioner and his site is a good starting place to learn about treating like with like. A Treat Yourself guide is included as are links to suppliers for online ordering.

Fragrant at Demon

http://www.fragrant.demon.co.uk/

Graham Sorenson's basic but unpretentious framed site is a good example of an individual using the web to promote an interest, hobby or business. It contains a list of UK aromatherapy practitioners and suppliers, a database with photos of people in Aromatherapy, descriptions of the oils used, a Symptoms Guide, Glossary, Events and a large annotated list of 600 other Aromatherapy sites. Clearly a work of love.

Hebsweb

http://www.hebs.scot.nhs.uk/

One day, all health sites will be like this. Conceived for and aimed at Scotland's appalling health problems, there is nonetheless something here for everyone – smoking, heart disease, healthy eating. There is an excellent Videowall facility (which requires a plug-in) and some of the site is for the health professions only. But the vast majority is accessible, useful, sobering and well-implemented.

Speed-up tip

Another way to System Tools – Right-click a drive in My Computer and then click Properties, Tools. Disk Cleanup, ScanDisk, Backup and Disk Defragmenter are available.

Kidshealth.org

http://kidshealth.org/

For kids, health is boring! However, the paediatric specialists at the Alfred I. duPont Hospital for Children in Florida understand this and have put together an excellent, attractive web site packed with information on infections, behaviour, emotions, food and fitness, and growing up healthy. They obviously understand children, as the games and animations show. A train theme leads to hundreds of articles and to-do features. If your kids must spend all their time and your phone bills playing net games, try them on this site and they might learn something. Also, subsites for parents and teenagers are worth a visit.

Medscape

http://www.medscape.com/index.html

If you want to annoy your GP, print out everything
there is to know on any condition from a Medline
search of the latest journals and go armed with the
information. This is a professionals' site available to
the public if you register. There is also an accessible
Patient Information section.

Parasol EMT

http://www.parasolemt.com.au/

This is an online First Aid information and advice
guide from Parasol, an Australian commercial
training provider of first aid and health and safety
training. It is Australia-focused, with a large section
on snakebites, but then eleven of the world's twelve
most venomous reptiles live there. Sensible,
pragmatic advice, easily searchable.

Speed-up tip

Performance improvement – If you have more than 16Mb of RAM, right-click on My Computer, Properties, Performance, File System, Hard disk, Typical Role of This Machine and change it to Network Server. Change Read-ahead optimisation to Full (drag the slider) and click OK. This increases the size of the file cache and thus speeds up the hard disk access. The change will take effect when you reboot. A power failure or other crash would be more likely to cause data loss in this setup, so use it only if you have a stable configuration with some form of backup power, or take the risk.

Patient Information

http://www.patient.co.uk/

It's your body, after all, so you should find out as much as possible about it. This is the place to start. There are about 20 categories of information and a wealth of links to other resources. As an exercise in collecting together and codifying the bewildering amount of information out there on the web, this site is truly excellent and devoid of pretentions.

Pharmweb

http://www.pharmweb.net/

This is a web site for professionals – pharmacists, doctors and others – and a lot of the information is technical and in depth. But for the general public there is an amazing amount of information on drugs and medicines. It is simply designed and easy to navigate if somewhat hard to read in places.

Quackwatch

http://www.quackwatch.com/

What a great idea. What a great name. Quackwatch unearths the frauds, fads and myths of alternative health. Researchers, doctors and users send their findings about the claims of conventional and unorthodox medicine from aromatherapy to cancer treatment. American psychiatrist Dr Stephen Barrett moderates the site. It's a good place to start before embarking on some unusual treatment.

Thrive Online

http://www.thriveonline.com/

This US site is a straghtfoward, no-nonsense
Consumer Health website packed with information
on medicine, fitness, sports, diet, and what they
coyly call passion. Online exercises, diets, medical
advice, etc. are worthwhile. Clear design and
multiple navigation options add to the site's appeal.

The Tooth Fairy

http://www.toothfairy.org/

Actually a site of links to other dental hygiene sites,
this nicely designed site is another good example of
an individual taking an obesssion online. It
provides access to a wealth of information on teeth
and tooth matters. I had no idea that oral disease
was recently shown to be the number one health
problem diagnosed in dogs and cats. In the USA,
perhaps.

Trashed

http://www.trashed.co.uk/audio/index.html

The Health Education Authority (HEA) used to be a worthy but boring organisation which tried to get us all to eat, behave and live more sensibly. This is video-enabled, sound-enabled, in-your-face information about drugs – their effects, the law, what's in them, emergencies and the risks. Trashed looks and feels like a rock video – they know their audience. A specially neat touch is the ability to tell them a new street name for a banned substance, so others can look it up. The HEA web site is at (http://www.hea.org.uk/).

Chapter Five

Non-Stop Shopping

AUCTIONS & WHOLESALE

Bottom Dollar
http://www.bottomdollar.com/

Ebay
http://www.ebay.com/

Excite's Product Finder
http://www.jango.com/xsh/index.dcg?

QXL
http://www.qxl.co.uk/

BOOKS

Chadwyck

http://lion.chadwyck.co.uk/html/homenosub.htm/

Chadwyck-Healey's Literature Online is a searchable database of over 260,000 works of English and American poetry, drama, and prose, plus biographies, bibliographies and key secondary sources and offers a free trial subscription plus deals for educational users.

Online Originals

http://www.onlineoriginals.com/

The Booker Prize, Britain's top fiction award, had a non-print entry in 1998 – Patricia le Roy's *The Angels of Russia*, published only on the web by Online Originals. If respectable, high-quality cyber-publishing ever takes off, Online Originals will be largely responsible.

MORE SITES TO SURF:

Amazon
http://www.amazon.co.uk/   http://www.amazon.com/

Barnes And Noble
http://www.barnesandnoble.com/

Books On Line
http://www.bol.com

The Book People
http://www.thebookpeople.co.uk/

Dillons
http://www.dillons.co.uk/

Heffers
http://www.heffers.co.uk/

Penguin
http://www.penguin.co.uk/

Internet tip

Disable the Active Desktop
– It's nice to be able to add
Web pages, news tickers
and other net stuff to your
desktop, but it does get in
the way processor-wise.
Right-click anywhere on the
desktop and tick or untick
Active Desktop.

CARS

Autobytel

http://www.autobytel.co.uk/

According to Autobytel one in five of us will choose
and buy a new car online by the end of 2001. They
have already sold more than two million cars
online in America. But what about the poor old
dealers? This site searches a UK database of new
and used vehicles, organises finance online and
emails orders to the nearest dealer, who delivers
(presumably not virtually).

Autohit

http://www.autohit.com/

This is the place to compare details and specifications of more than 3,000 car models, and has good reviews. Buy elsewhere, though.

Autolocate

http://autolocate.uk.msn.com/

Time for a new-reg car? This site allows the car-seeking surfer to locate new and used cars from dealers in the UK. There are two search modes – one which allows specification of make, model, price and distance from your postcode, and the second a Wizard which guides you through the same process. It appears to access over 500 dealers.

Internet tip

Don't waste time – If things take forever, hit the Stop button (or Back).

Carseekers

http://www.carseekers.co.uk/

They find your car in Europe, often 30% cheaper than at home. Then they ship it for you. Appallingly designed site, but at £3,000 off your next Mondeo, who cares? Registration is required, however.

Classic Cars World

http://www.classiccarsworld.co.uk/

Old banger or sought-after classic? This web site, based on the famous mag of similar name, will show you how to tell the difference and even how to convert one into the other. The events calendar is good.

COMPUTERS

Dabs Direct
http://www.dabs.com/

Dan Technology
http://www.dan.co.uk/

Dell
http://www.dell.co.uk/

Elonex
http://www.elonex.co.uk/

Evesham Micros
http://www.evesham.com/

Insight
http://www.insight.com/uk/

Pico Direct
http://www.picodirect.co.uk/

Tech Direct
http://www.techdirect.co.uk/

Dixons/Curry's
http://www.dixons.com/

Internet tip

Don't waste more time – While a page is downloading, hit Ctrl-N to start a new window and pursue another link.

Someone given you a web page with no way to close it? Use Alt + F4.

FOOD & DRINK

Chateau Online
http://www.chateauonline.co.uk/

The Classic England Shopping Mall
http://www.classicengland.co.uk/

Fortnum And Mason
http://www.fortnumandmason.co.uk/

Jayfruit
http://www.jayfruit.co.uk/

Thorntons Online
http://www.thorntons.co.uk/

Wine Cellar UK
http://www.winecellar.co.uk/

Sainsburys Online

http://www.sainsburys.co.uk/orderline/main.asp

One day I will bite the bullet and have all my groceries delivered from an online order rather than walk the 400 metres to Tesco. If I do, I may well choose Sainsburys. It is well-designed, fast and easy to navigate. The catch? They don't deliver to my area. Is it raining out?

MORE SITES TO SURF:

Tesco

http://www.tesco.co.uk/

Boots

http://www.boots.co.uk/

Waitrose

http://www.waitrose.com/

Internet tip

Faster browsing – If typing in a URL, start from www. onwards and your browser will fill in the http:// automatically.

And often you don't need to type the starting page.

HOME & INTERIORS

Craftdesign

http://www.craftdesign-london.com/

A design site should have a good design, so that's all right, then. Contemporary British design for the home is featured, with examples from accessories, ceramics, furniture, glassware, metalwork and tableware and designers such as Samantha Broady and Taylor & Parr.

Feng Shui

http://www.online-fengshui.com/

Pronounced *fung*, meaning sense and *shway*, more money than. Is your house the right way round? Improve your health, wealth and happiness. Find the part of the room that has money-bringing energy and the best place to conceive a child (probably not the same).

Sotheby's

http://www.sothebys.com/

This outstanding site features the expected know-how and collectors' advice as well as interactive adventures. There are also excellent sections on auctions, auction results and schedules, collecting in general, a gallery guide, glossary, online catalogues, a search service, information on tax, trusts and estates, a good history section and more besides. The design is also well-conceived and the navigation helpful.

Internet tip

Display link filenames –
Hover your mouse over a
link and see its URL in the
status line at bottom of the
screen. Right click and copy

shortcut will put the URL
onto the clipboard. Paste it
into a Notebook file for
later use.

DESIGNER SHOPPING

Bras Direct
http://www.brasdirect.co.uk/bras/

Charles Tyrwhitt
http://www.ctshirts.co.uk/

Diesel UK
http://www.diesel.co.uk

Levi
http://www.eu.levi.com/

FAO Schwartz
http://www.faoschwartz.com/

Gap
http://www.gap.com/

Macy's

http://www.macys.com/

Scotia

http://www.scotia.uk.com/

INTERNET SHOPPING

Buy

http://www.buy.co.uk/

A simple if unimaginative design fronts a good deal
of information on internet shopping. There are
comparisons of phone, electric, gas, water and
mobile phone charges. An email reminder system
can inform you of sales and a Business Purchasing
service is promised soon.

Internet tip

Hot links – Right-click on a hyperlink and drag it to a clear place on your desktop, and you'll have a shortcut that opens your browser and navigates straight to the linked page. Shortcuts can be moved to a folder or dragged to a document or email message.

Richclickings

http://www.richclickings.com/

Straightforward reviews and links to over 400 shops featuring, among others, organic food, additive-free food and wholefood sites, many of which are American. It also has the Top 20 UK online shops (but doesn't say by what criteria) and had a boycott of online French shops at the time when that mattered.

Shoppers Universe

http://www.shoppersuniverse.com/

GUS is the granddaddy (or is it Great Aunt) of catalogue shopping and this is the online version. Claims to be The shopping mall for the whole world are therefore a bit stretched, but it has a useful place. However, it absolutely requires that you accept a cookie, which many of us are uncomfortable with.

SECOND-HAND

Preloved

http://www.preloved.co.uk/index.cfm

This is a second-hand sales site with everything from holidays to houseboats. Become an affiliate and you effectively host a buy-anything service on your site, with a cut of each sale for you.

Chapter Six

Managing Your Money

Banking Review

http://www.bankreview.org.uk/

You may not be fascinated by the Review of Banking Services in the UK, but this independent investigation of banking is looking at innovation, competition and efficiency in the industry and how well it serves the needs of business, consumers and the UK economy. All the working documents and the final report will be available on this site, which will also take responses during the consultation process. This is open government at its best.

Web tip

Design tip – watch your colours – When you design a web page, you cannot guarantee that someone else's browser will render all your carefully chosen colours exactly. To avoid this, stick to the Netscape 216-colour pallette.

Businessman's Guide To Europe   BUSINESS

http://europa.eu.int/en/comm/dg23/guide_en/index2.htm

Bewildered by Europe? Wondering what help there is out there? Where are all the lucrative EU contracts, grants and projects? All is revealed in this site. There is also a link to other EU Member State official sites and an excellent search engine.

Companies in Banking & Finance   BANKING

http://www.mrweb.co.uk/dotcom/fina-co.htm

It may not seem like much, but this simple page of links has the web site of your bank, building society, credit card company, merchant bank and accountant. A useful, helpful web resource. Thanks, Mr Web.

Consumer Info   FINANCE

http://www.consumerinfo.com/index.html

How's your credit rating? If you don't know, lots of
other people do, including anyone you apply to for
finance, insurance, credit cards, etc. Sign up for a
free 30-day trial, and you receive a credit report. If
you continue, the CreditCheck Monitoring Service
will send you information on your credit. You will
know everything credit checkers know. Comforting,
isn't it?

Fidelity Investments   BUSINESS

http://www.fidelity.co.uk/

This is the UK arm of **http://www.fidelity.com** which
was instrumental in forcing the acceptance of
virtual signature technology, which allows you to
(for instance) open accounts via the internet and
move money around. There are also facilities to
review investments and look at fund performance.
There is far more going on behind this site than at
first appears.

Web tip

Design tip – watch your fonts – Use standard fonts (Arial, Helvetica, Times New Roman, etc.) which other browsers will have loaded. Otherwise your page may not display the way you intended. A common combination is a Serif font (like Times New Roman) for headings and a Sans Serif font (Arial, Helvetica, etc.) for body text. Remember also that not everyone will have your favourite Alaska ExtraBold Italic loaded on their own PCs. Use a bright coloured font against a dark background (or vice versa) and you can often get away with a smaller font size.

HM Treasury   BUSINESS

http://www.hm-treasury.gov.uk/

It's your money. Here is where to get the latest reports, press releases and other information put forth by the Treasury on economic and financial matters.

Inland Revenue   TAX

http://www.inlandrevenue.gov.uk/

Now and again, someone you would absolutely not
expect gets it absolutely right. The tax site is a
delight. Hector the Inspector (the cute pinstriped
character from the TV adverts) is your guide to self-
assessment, with all the forms and guides online
and downloadable. It even starts Good afternoon.
Lovely. And I know at least one otherwise sensible
and boring Chartered Accountant who gets great
fun out of the Beat The Taxman screen saver. Either
the Revenue has finally hired someone with a
sense of humour or the web designers deserve
a medal. They appear not to deserve a
mention, which is a pity.

Web tip

Design tip: bigger files take longer – Our company logo may be super-duper, all-dancing animation and cost an arm and a leg from the multimedia mob downstairs, but who is going to wait a minute or more to see it? You can reduce file sizes by cutting down the number of colours. If your graphics must have lots of colours, save them as jpg files. If not, use gif. Specify an optimised palette. Only use the resolution you need – the typical computer screen displays at 96 dpi or less.

Interactive Investor   SHARES

http://www.iii.co.uk/

This is aimed more at the serious investor and can search company share prices, independent financial advisers and the performance of investment funds. A lot of it is reserved for registered users but a surprising amount of information is free, including some extremely readable guides to investment. There are links to related sites dealing with PEPs, offshore investments and the like. The Net Community facilities and forums are interesting.

Web tip

Design tip – use Alt text –
A useful aspect of graphics on the web is that they can have Alt (alternative) text associated with them; this displays text while the graphic is loading and when the mouse cursor passes over it. But make it something meaningful, like 'Map of Tonga' not just wdfr1462.gif

Legal & General

INSURANCE

http://www.landg.com/

This insurance company was among the first to take the web seriously and has won a number of prestigious awards for handing control back to the user. Track your mortgage payments, take out medical insurance and find out where your nearest Approved Hospital is. The site is bright, attractive and easy to use. Note the .com address, part of a trend by UK companies to look more international by avoiding the .co.uk ending, which is reckoned to have a provincial feel to it and scare off the lucrative US market.

Internet tip

Browse offline – Browsing the web can be slow but Internet Explorer 4 and 5 let you work offline and browse via the cache. Select File, Work Offline to disconnect and you can read files directly from your hard drive. If a page hasn't stored in your cache, you see a small 'not' sign next to the cursor. If you click a link that connects to a page not in your cache, you get the options of either going online to retrieve the page or staying offline.

Moneyworld   FINANCE

http://www.moneyworld.co.uk/

This is one of the best introductions to personal finance available anywhere. There are guides to important aspects like mortgages and pensions, a good news service, a large directory of financial institutions, share prices and excellent consumer information. The inevitable advertisers offer discounts and there are links to the web sites of most UK finance houses. It looks businesslike and is very easy to use but hard to get lost in.

National Savings

FINANCE

http://www.nationalsavings.co.uk/

Think you might have a Premium Bond that came
up trumps but you didn't know about it? Search
Ernie online to find out. This is a good example of
an attractive web site used to front a dull but
worthy subject, including the tax rules on the
bewildering variety of National Savings products,
ISAs and how to invest.

Quote.com

SHARES

http://www.quote.com

How are your shares doing? Quote can tell you.
There is an interesting symbol lookup facility (since
nobody can remember what their favourite share's
symbol is), plus company snapshots, an excellent
series of charts and the opportunity
to build a My Portfolio query
which will report on your own
batch of holdings. Simple to use
yet extensive in its reach,
Quote.com is the web at its best.

Internet tip

Browse local HTML files – You can browse web page files on your hard disk. Enter URLs like:

file:///users/USER/public_html/index.html in your browser's address box.

Screentrade   INSURANCE

http://www.screentrade.co.uk/

It doesn't take a genius to figure out that if replacing insurance and pensions salesmen with call centre operators cuts costs and makes for cheaper products, then taking the whole insurance brokering service online is the next logical step. There is no guarantee that the prices quoted here are always the lowest, but what is it worth not to be on the end of one of those interminable phone calls while sorting out your car cover? This is online shopping at its best, for services you would be buying anyway.

Wall Street Journal: Money and Investing Update

SHARES

`http://update.wsj.com/`

What can I say – it's the *Wall Street Journal*. There is a subscription option, but a lot of information on this busy and businesslike web site is free.

Wells Fargo Bank

BANKING

`http://www.wellsfargo.com`

I do confess – if I lived in the USA I would bank with Wells Fargo. Not only do they give you a chequebook with pictures of stage coaches all over it, they have by far the most exciting web site of any bank. There are stories from Wells Fargo's history, an interactive museum with photos and paintings of the wild west, and every day a true story from the company's colourful past. This is an excellent resource for teachers, students and Louis Lamour fans everywhere. It makes you want to put on a mask and go hold up a train. Yee-Hah!

Chapter Seven

Amusing the Kids

Argo Sphere

http://www.argosphere.net

Activities organised by age ranges offer interactive elements for children, parents and teachers. After registration, the free part of this web site can be accessed and has a great deal of interesting and valuable content.

Atlapedia Online

http://www.atlapedia.com/index.html

Visit here for information on every country in the world with facts, figures and statistics on geography, climate, people, religion, language, history and economy. A World Maps area has full colour physical and political maps.

Speed-up tip

*Improve your memory –
enable RAM cacheing –*
Memory performance is
critical in Windows 95 and
98. If your system is slow,
check your BIOS settings to
ensure the memory cache is
not disabled. The specific
names of the BIOS settings
vary depending on the
manufacturer, but are
usually something like
Enable Internal Cache,
Enable CPU Cache or
Disable/Enable L1 Cache. To
get to the BIOS, restart the
computer and wait for a
message saying 'Hit DEL to
enter BIOS' or something
similar. Then do it. Be
careful in the BIOS – don't
change anything you don't
understand and hit ESC to
leave without saving, if
you're worried.

BBC Education

http://www.bbc.co.uk/education

You can't beat the Beeb. Start at the Schools Online
area with Bitesize revision help, spin off into the
Learning Zone, follow up on a TV or radio
programme, check out related items in the News
pages and don't forget to send an email to *Blue
Peter*.

Beano

http://www.beano.co.uk/

Yaroo! *The Beano* just won't go away. This site has all the favourites plus games and things to do in a colourful, easy-to-use format.

Britannia

http://britannia.com/

This huge site is put together in America using UK contributors. For schools, the History (http://britannia.com/history) and Monarchy (http://britannia.com/monarchy) sections will be especially useful, with excellent maps, timelines, features and images. Many a school project could start and finish in this site alone.

Speed-up tip

Free up disc space – Empty your Recycle bin – right-click on the desktop Recycle Bin icon, select Empty Recycle Bin and click

OK. This is better than deleting files from the recycle bin folder in Explorer.

CIA Kids Page

http://www.odci.gov/cia/ciakids/safe.html

I just had to put it in. This is the friendly, cuddly face of the world's largest intelligence organisation with a Kids' Secret Zone. Make your own judgement.

Cybersitter   SECURITY

http://www.solidoak.com/

This is a cheap, reliable filter which sits in the background, blocks disallowed access and maintains a history list. Look out kids – your parents know where you've been!

Cyber Teen

http://www.cteen.com/

News for teens who want to know. Parents keep out!

Dark Knight

http://www.darkknight.ca/dknight.html

Admirers of gaudy heroic iconography will find much to admire (and download) at The Dark Knight with its excellent interactives, while aspiring comics writers will pore over DC Comics Submission Guidelines (http://www.dccomics.com/guides/guides.htm). For collectors, the best place is Collecting Comics (http://www.collecting-comics.com/museum/default.asp). This Comic Book Museum showcases the greatest comic books from hard-to-find examples of the 40s and 50s to current favourites. Visitors can add their own comics to the database and buy/sell/trade by email. Oh, why did I give all of mine away?

> ## Speed-up tip
>
> ***Free up more disc space***
> – You can safely delete any
> file with the extensions .bak
> or .old, unless you need
> them for some special
> purpose (like a backup copy
> of a system file), or any file
> beginning with a ~ symbol.

Fishydance

http://www.fishydance.com/index.htm

This is a site with no point whatsoever – pictures of
fish dancing to a tune of your choice. Pick 'Fish
Heads' for the best of these. Then go quietly mad.

Infant Explorer

http://www.naturegrid.org.uk/infant/

Sebastian the Swan is your guide to literacy through
stories and Big Books with an environmental bent.
This would make a good basis for environment
projects in schools. A really good feature is the
Secret Agent tool which explains how to browse the
site offline, from cache memory.

Kidsclick!

http://sunsite.berkeley.edu/KidsClick!/

The Berkeley Digital Library (see p.109) has
catalogued more than 3,500 web resources for
children, all carefully chosen, described and
organised. Not to mention the cute aliens. Once
you let your children near this site, you may never
see them again!

Kinderart

http://www.kinderart.com/lessons.htm

This web site is huge. It contains a massive
collection of artistic lessons including how to make
art materials from household items and a weekly
activity, quizzes and interactive elements. A great
resource for Art teachers in schools and a superb aid
to creativity.

Speed-up tip

Free up more disc space still – Your Windows system accumulates a lot of temporary files as a result of system crashes, bad shutdowns, failed installations and the like. Last time I checked I found 846 .TMP files in my c:/Windows/Temp folder, all zero-length. Close all open programs, open Explorer, find the TEMP directory and delete all files with a .TMP extension. Click on the Type or Size tab to order the files (all the TMP files or all zero-length files together, for instance). If Windows does not allow you to delete a file, leave it – it may be in use.

Mathsnet

http://www.anglia.co.uk/education/mathsnet

Hats off to Anglia for putting together this attractive admixture of downloadable software, puzzles, games, interactive activities, feature articles and two good indexes (alphabetical and nested). Struggling with maths? Really into numbers? There is something in this web site for everyone.

NASA Kids

http://kids.earth.nasa.gov/

NASA's kids site about the earth explains the greenhouse effect, El Nino, plate tectonics and space.

National Geographic

http://www.nationalgeographic.com/kids

A subsite of the highly recommended National Geographic web, this children's area is packed with information, links to reference tools, a pen pal network, Amazing Facts, a cartoon factory and a games/activity area.

Net Nanny   SECURITY

http://www.netnanny.com/

This program filters content and can also prevent data from going out onto the web, such as your address, phone and other personal and sensitive information.

Speed-up tip

Launch your applications faster – Convert your hard disk to FAT32 using Start, Programs, Accessories, System Tools, Drive converter, then run the Maintenance wizard from Start, Programs, Accessories, System Tools. BACK UP EVERYTHING FIRST!

Nimby

http://www.notinmybackyard.com/

Nicely designed as a framed cartoon with clickable links, this site has some intruiging features – the Artist link leads to one of the strangest but most effective rollover graphics on the web. The Doghouse has clipart and colouring activities for children.

Nine Planets

http://seds.lpl.arizona.edu/billa/tnp/

Bill Arnett's wonderful site shows the planets and major moons in the solar system. Rich with still images, movies and sounds, this feels like a real space voyage. There is also an index of images.

Planetary Photojournal

http://photojournal.jpl.nasa.gov/

This is a collection of many of the best images from NASA's planetary exploration program, indexed by planet and exploration vehicle. Most are available in gif or jpg format. Plus there is lots of information about each of the planets. Check out Saturn's rings and moons.

Robots In Space

http://www.brookes.ac.uk/rms/robots

Recommended for 11–13-year-olds, this subsite of Oxford Brookes University's web lets children explore robots, their construction and their functions in space with guidance from robots Mervyn and Robert. The site uses frames, Java and Shockwave Flash, so get the latest browser and plug-ins. Some illustrations require 3-D glasses – although there is a good explanation of how to use coloured sweet papers. Good links to other robot sites.

RSAC   SECURITY

http://www.rsac.org

The Recreational Software Advisory Council (RSAC)
was established, with the support of Microsoft, IBM,
Disney and others, to provide ratings for web and
internet content and uses the Platform for Internet
Content Selection (PICS) infrastructure to provide
ratings on sites. This site has information on RSAC,
navigation to other pages which allow rating,
registration of your web site and reports on relevant
topics.

The Rubber Chicken

http://www.rubberchicken.com/

This is the place for practical jokes and other gags.
There are also numerous links to other like-minded
sites.

University and College Maps

http://www.scit.wlv.ac.uk/ukinfo/uk.map.html

Looking for a College or University to go to? The
University of Wolverhampton maintains a site with
clickable maps of universities, HE colleges, FE and
other colleges and research centres. Clicking takes
you directly to particular places' own web sites. A
very useful resource for post-school education
generally.

WWWaste Of Time

http://www.accessv.com/~georged/WWWasteofTime

Dedicated to the noble pursuit of wasting
everybody's time online, the site lives up to its
name. A neat feature is a 'Here Comes The Boss!'
hyperlink to a real commercial web site. Or not. It's
your risk. Who said the Canadians had no sense of
humour?

Yahooligans!

http://www.yahooligans.com/

The youth and school-age version of search engine Yahoo! presents lists and links for content suitable for younger surfers, with nested categories so that children can easily find subjects of interest. There are also events and reference areas, but with a US bias. Still, it is worthwhile as a starting place for all ages.

Chapter Eight

Fun Learning

Acronym Dictionary

REFERENCE

http://www.ucc.ie/info/net/acronyms/index.html

Search for an acronym or a word. Basic design and functionality, but it works (except in some beta versions of version 4 browsers).

Allexperts.com

REFERENCE

http://www.allexperts.com/

This is the web at its best – more than 3,500 volunteer experts will answer any question on any topic. This is better than using Newsgroups since here you may ask a specific question of a specialist you select, which includes mechanics, doctors, gardeners, cooks, educationalists, travel experts and even God, apparently.

Explorer tip

Change groups to folders – Windows 3.1 kept programs together in groups, while Windows 95 and 98 use desktop folders. If you have useful Win 3.1 groups (all your graphics programs for instance) you can convert these to Win 9x folders. There are two ways to do this. 1. Click a .grp file to automatically convert it. 2. Start, Run and type in GRPCONV /m to display a dialog box. Browse for .grp files to convert first.

Alt.Culture   REFERENCE

http://www.altculture.com/

Youth culture is elegantly expressed in this encyclopaedia of recent times aimed at teenagers. The design reflects the audience with bright colours, strong visuals and easy navigation – including a 'random search' feature which produces a blizzard of information. This could just be the place for parents who don't understand their children.

Antcam
BIOLOGY

http://antcam.nhm.ac.uk/antcast.html

Bored with night views over the Volga? Then watch this infrared webcamera at the Natural History Museum's leafcutter ant farm. Antfacts also feature. Not one for the formiphobes.

Bartlett's
REFERENCE

http://www.columbia.edu/acis/bartleby/bartlett/

Bartlett's Familiar Quotations is well known so Columbia University, New York, established Project Bartleby to take it (and other valuable literary and reference publications) online. Browsing and searching are easy and the design is simple yet effective.

Explorer tip

Using SendTo – If you have shortcuts to a printer, fax, network drive, Windows program, My Briefcase, email, etc., drag the shortcut to the SendTo folder (in the C:/ Windows folder). To open the folder, click Start, Run, type SendTo in the Open box and press ENTER. The right mouse button can drag an item's icon into the SendTo window and the shortcut appears in the SendTo menu. To send a document or folder right-click the icon, click Send To and click the appropriate menu item. For instance, create a link to your Fax program in the SendTo folder. Then right-click a document and click SendTo and Fax to send it.

Berkeley Digital Library   REFERENCE

http://sunsite.berkeley.edu/

The combination of a large university and a large computer company ought to make for a fast and worthwhile site and that is precisely what the BDL is. Textual material, images, oral history and a wealth of other material is available from keyword searches at a remarkable speed. The site links to similar libraries around the world.

BugClub

ENTOMOLOGY

http://www.ex.ac.uk/bugclub/

One for the My Little Entomologist brigade with excellent features and facts on creepy crawlies.

The Calendar

TIME

http://155.135.31.26/oliver/smt310-handouts/calendar.htm

Why do we have the calendar we have? This basic but information-packed site has all the answers.

Calendar Conversions

TIME

http://genealogy.org/~scottlee/calconvert.cgi

While you're at it, what date is it in the Julian, Jewish or French republican calendar system? This conversion site will tell you.

Web tip

Domains registered as plc must be PLCs – You will have to provide evidence in the form of a Company Registration Number or similar documentation and demonstrate that you are entitled to use the name. Others such as .edu, .ac and .gov are reserved for special purposes (education, academic and government) and the likes of us can't get them. The .com, .net and .org domain suffixes indicate 'global' domains because they are not affiliated with any country. Anyone from anywhere can register a .com, .net or .org domain. You can register as many as you wish, as long as you pay the fees. These are 'top-level domains' in the domain name system. New domain names (.tv, .shop, .firm, .arts, .rec, .info and .nom) are on the way.

Center for Scientific Computing

BIOCHEMISTRY

http://www.csc.fi:80/lul/chem/graphics.html

CSC hosts a chemical art gallery full of images of electrons, atoms, molecules, proteins and polymers. Science as art has never been so well represented as here. Some of the images may require special plug-ins or viewers.

CERN

PHYSICS

http://wwwas.cern.ch/OpenDay/PressOffice/Index.html

The European Laboratory for Particle Physics is the world's largest research centre. The web site offers a vast range of downloadable nuclear physics images and links to other relevant information.

Clementine

SPACE

http://www.nrl.navy.mil/clementine/

This site has an excellent range of images and animations of the Moon and Earth from the Clementine spacecraft as well as an online catalogue of the exhibit of Clementine imagery at the National Academy of Sciences.

Explorer tip

Make Explorer open at different folders – Start, Programs, Explorer starts exploring from the boot drive. Right-Click Start, Explorer starts in \Windows\StartMenu. Right-Click My Computer, Explore starts browsing in My Computer. Click My Computer, hold down Shift, Double-click on My Computer again – this starts from a collapsed tree. Try them!

Colorado State University   ENTOMOLOGY

http://www.colostate.edu/Depts/Entomology/images.html

Given that there are over one million species of parasitic wasps alone, there is no chance that any entomological image collection will be complete. But the departments of Entomology at CSU and at Iowa State (below) have a good try. CSU hosts an extensive collection of images of insects, arthropods and their relatives. The indexing is clear, even for those untrained in taxonomy. The movies of various insects are interesting.

Dictionary.Com
REFERENCE

http://www.dictionary.com/

Apart from the expected look-up function (which
annoys me, since an old teacher of mine would
never tell us the spelling of a word but say 'look it
up', but if you don't know how to spell it, how do
you... never mind) there is also the same Word of
the Day and Crossword shared with stablemate
Roget.com and much more. This is the only
dictionary in which I have ever found a definition
for 'coadunate'.

Encarta Online
REFERENCE

http://encarta.msn.com/EncartaHome.asp

For those without access to Encarta (Microsoft's
computer-based encyclopaedia) on CD-ROM or
over a network, the 'concise' is available free with a
fee-based full search option. There are puzzles,
quizzes, educational games and good visuals
including some 360° views.

Web tip

Find out if your domain name is available – For a .com domain, go to Network Solutions (http://www.networksolutions.com/) who will tell you if the name is available, and if not, suggest alternatives. Other search services are Ask Reggie (http://askreggie.com/ and use the International Search for .co.uk, etc.); Internic (http://www.internic.net/) which is the international domain naming body; and Easyspace (http://www.easyspace.com/) who may have deals.

Encyclopedia.com   REFERENCE

http://www.encyclopedia.com/

I shall be in a minority of one here, but I prefer this to Britannica. It consists of 14,000 entries from the Concise Columbia Electronic Encyclopedia. Infonauts (no, it's not in dictionary.com) amongst us will admire the predictable but nicely executed book-page format which is grouped alphabetically.

Web tip

Start at a search engine –
Every journey starts with a
single step. On the Web, it's
usually a search. Any one of
these search engine main

pages could be set up as
your browser's Home Page
so that it is your first point
of contact each time you
log on.

Florence Webcam   REFERENCE

http://www.vps.it/florence/

Apart from the live cam there is good information
on Florentine history back to Roman times.

Friends Of The Earth Scotland   ENVIRONMENT

http://www.foe-scotland.org.uk/

Environmental activists start here – although the
site is slow to load (easy to fix, FOE!) it is packed
with information on campaigns, briefing
documents and extensive links to like-minded
bodies. Particularly good are the sections on Get
Your Beach Protected, sustainable use of resources
in Europe and schools projects.

Web tip

Get a domain name – This is the heart of your internet identity. It is your brand for online activities and is unique to you. In technical terms a domain name is an alias. Computers use Internet Protocol (IP) numbers to locate each other on the internet, of the form 127.123.456.789, but these are hard to remember and hardly as user-friendly as www.shoeshop.com or whatever you have chosen.

Greenpeace   ENVIRONMENT

http://www.greenpeace.org.uk/

This clear and unstrident site has all the updates on GM foods, the nuclear test ban treaty, oil exploration and other environmental issues around the world.

The Internet Public Library   REFERENCE

http://ipl.sils.umich.edu/

One of the great libraries on your (virtual) doorstep.

Web tip

Links can go away – Check your links often to make sure the sites or pages haven't gone away or been moved.

Isbister   EARTH SCIENCES

http://www.isbister.com/worldtime/index.html

If you need to know the exact time anywhere on Earth, Isbister (makers of time management software) have a free site which will tell you to the second. This is great for synchronising your Windows clock.

Lawrence Livermore Laboratory   ENERGY

http://www.llnl.gov/graphics/images_clips.html

Science sees things we don't, by using special imaging techniques. The scientific visualisation site has pictures of such esoteric concepts as flow volumes, textured splats, line bundles, spot noise and unstructured volume data texture rendering.

Web tip

Register a .co.uk domain –
To register a.co.uk domain,
go to Nominet
(http://www.nic.uk/), a non-
profit making company
who only register UK-based
companies, organisations
and individuals. If you are
not in the UK, find a
registrar based in your
country that you can trust.
It will be easier to deal with
them on the phone if
everything doesn't go
according to plan.

Medline   MEDICINE

http://www.nlm.nih.gov

The US National Library of Medicine's portal to all
aspects of medicine. Includes a search facility,
puckishly titled 'Grateful Med', which accesses a
number of huge databases including the wonderful
Spaceline, a collection of information on space
medicine and the effects of low gravity on human
physiology. PubMed has access to 9 million medical
citations including complete genome sequences and
Medline Plus contains consumer health
information. This is the most complete medical
reference source available anywhere.

Merriam-Webster's Dictionary   REFERENCE

http://www.m-w.com/

I cannot resist a dictionary with jokes.
Apart from this being one of the web's
best word resources, The Lighter Side
of Language deserves special mention.
I simply did not know that the
Sanskrit root pardate figured in my
everyday speech or that Shakespeare
coined the word leapfrog. The design
is straightforward, fast and easy on the eye. Give
someone a prize, please.

Met Office   WEATHER

http://www.met-office.gov.uk/

Unlike some UK government sites, this one is well-
organised, designed for clarity and fast. General
forecast, up-to-the-minute reports by city or region,
advanced forecasts and shipping warnings all
feature.

Explorer tip

Drag to copy – You can drag a file to move it but hold the Ctrl-key while you drag and it will copy a file to the new folder.

NASA

SPACE

http://www.hq.nasa.gov/office/pao/Library/photo.html

NASA has compiled a large gallery of images of the solar system, the Earth and its oceans, flight vehicles, robotics, aeronautical and space flight equipment, and mission patches. A video gallery (http://www.hq.nasa.gov/office/pao/Library/video.html) includes footage shot from space vehicles, satellite views of hurricanes and monsoons and live NASA TV.

National Oceanic and Atmospheric Administration

ENERGY

http://www.graysreef.nos.noaa.gov/pictures.html

NOAA's Gray's Reef National Marine Sanctuary has a superb collection of underwater images. Just like a trip in a glass-bottomed boat.

Web tip

Register a domain name – If you know what you want your domain name to be, you can register it and join the other 4 million domain name owners. If you are not ready to go online with a web site just yet, you can reserve a domain, thereby protecting your internet brand until it is ready to use. Do not delay – domain names disappear fast, either because someone else has the same idea and gets in first, or because someone will speculatively register it.

Nature   GENERAL

http://www.nature.com/

Register (free) and you have access to the world's most authoritative science news resource. This will allow searches, browsing of the tables of contents and first paragraphs and a free weekly email summary of *Nature*'s contents. Subscribing brings more benefits, including linking from references to abstracts in the ISI and Medline databases. There are also science job adverts and a link to an international grants register for fund seekers.

Web tip

Choosing your domain name – Letters, numbers and hyphens can be used but you cannot begin or end a domain name with a hyphen. So my-site.com is fine, but -mysite.com is not. Spaces, apostrophes ('), exclamation marks (!) and underscores (_), are not allowed in web addresses – jim's great_site!.co.uk would fail for all four reasons. However, you can have some special characters in file names: mysite.com/start_here.htm would be OK if your server allows it – some do, some don't.

NCAR

EARTH SCIENCES

http://www.mmm.ucar.edu/

The National Center for Atmospheric Research has a wealth of information on Earth's atmosphere and interesting visuals. Particularly good is the water vapour imagery from the GOES-8 satellite and the more general gallery of satellite images.

Nobel Prize Internet Archive GENERAL

http://nobelprizes.com/nobel/nobel.html

Who won what, when, and for what? What did
Einstein actually do? Relevant information and
other literature and other resources are all here. And
for more on Albert himself, browse Albert Einstein
Online (**http://www.firstmonday.dk/issues/issue2_2/
friedman/#dep1**).

NPR Science Friday Kids
Connection GENERAL

http://www.npr.org/programs/sfkids/

National Public Radio is the only US equivalent of
our own Radio. Much of its scientific radio output
suitable for school-age children is available in a
sound archive, a lot of it featuring the world's
second-greatest science journalist, Joe Palca.

Web tip

Free email accounts – Many ISPs offer free email accounts (often 5, but sometimes unlimited). A small company might need one per employee or a home user one for each family member. Usually, an email account is easy to set up with software configuration done over the web (known as webmail). In these cases you will be stuck with the host's domain name – your email address from Freethingy may become mmouse@freethingy.net, but if you have also taken some web space you may get a virtual domain to yourself, with a name you choose, such as mmouse@mousehole.freeth ingy.net.

Phrase Finder   REFERENCE

`http://www.shu.ac.uk/web-admin/phrases/go.html`

A database of 6,000 phrases can be searched by single word, or browsed by an A–Z list. The list of phrases complete with their meanings and derivations is interesting. Surfers can also contribute meanings and derivations. Thanks to me, they now know the etymology of 'Berk'.

Physics News Graphics

PHYSICS

http://www.aip.org/physnews/graphics

The American Institute of Physics maintains an
archive of images on physics-related topics. They
also host the Emilio Segre Visual Archives
(http://www.aip.org/history/esva), a collection of
photographs and biographies of physicists past and
present.

Roget's Thesaurus

REFERENCE

http://www.thesaurus.com

This is an excellent example of how having a useful
publication available online makes it even more
useful. The great utility of Roget is to use a word to
find other words of similar, related or different
meaning. This is so much easier by computer than
on paper. Entries can be accessed alphabetically or
by categories. There are also word games and
crossword puzzles.

Web tip

If your ISP registers your domain – Your ISP may register your domain name for you and charge you the appropriate fee. For instance, ConnectFree (http://www.connectfree.co.uk/) will provide free registration for a domain name of your choice for .co.uk and .org names (actually, it costs a three-minute phone call at £1.50 per minute plus £5 every two years). Their site includes a Search facility to determine if the domain name is free. They will charge you £25 if you subsequently move the domain name to another host.

Sciencedirect   GENERAL

http://www.sciencedirect.com/

Elsevier's site offers access to more than 1,000 scientific, technical and medical journals and publications. There is also an excellent set of links to other science resources, mainly aimed at working research scientists, but worthwhile for a general scan, too.

Science Magazine   GENERAL

http://www.sciencemag.org/

Browse, search and read current articles or the
archive of America's prime science publication. The
most useful feature is the Hot Picks – the best of
science, prechosen, with links. Like Nature (above)
there is an email updating service. Science is aimed
at professionals, but ScienceNow
(http://www.sciencenow.org/) is its online public
service, including a good historical and archive
section, Science Then.

Stanford Visible Female   MEDICINE

http://summit.stanford.edu/RESEARCH/StanfordVisibleFe
male/images.html

For the gynaecologist in all of us, the Stanford
Visible Female site has 3-D images of a
cryopreserved female pelvis, should you need such a
thing.

Web tip

***Website directories* –** Directories are not the same as search engines, although they usually include these. If you don't mind someone else's ideas of what sites to be sent to (which often comes down to who has paid to be there) then AltaVista'a Looksmart is as good as any.

Visible Human Project   MEDICINE

http://www.nlm.nih.gov/research/visible/visible_human.
html#viewers

The Visible Human is an ambitious project to render a body as a data set. This site provides links to various visualisation projects using these data.

Women In Technology International   GENERAL

http://www.witi.com/cgi-bin/check.cgi

Anyone with an interest in women's issues in science should start here. There are online magazines, news, information on women in science and technology jobs, forums, chat places and events.

World Climate   WEATHER

`http://www.worldclimate.com/`

Instantaneous weather reports are a fine thing if
you're leaving tomorrow. But what will the weather
be like in Maui next October? This site has average
monthly temperatures and rainfall for thousands of
places so you can have some confidence that your
bargain break in Bali is cheap because it's the
monsoon season.

WWW Virtual Library   REFERENCE

`http://www.mth.uea.ac.uk/VL`

There is a nice contrast here between the
'professionals for amateurs' approach of Allexperts
(above) and this 'professionals for professionals'
service. Aimed at academics, it is serviced by experts
who research and provide lists of key links to their
areas of expertise. There are six mirror sites
internationally, including the University of East
Anglia, which has made a virtue of providing web-
based educational resources.

Web tip

Download an image for your web site – Right-click (PC) or click and hold (Mac), then select 'Save Image As...' (Netscape) or 'Save Picture As...' (Internet Explorer). You can change the name if you wish. Save the image in the folder where you keep your own web page files. Edit your web page and place the image where you like. Never use an image without permission, unless it is public domain.

Yucky   ENTOMOLOGY

http://www.yucky.com/

This is for the less scientifically minded than BugClub (above) – send buggy email cards to your pals and show your parents the simplified Guide to the web.

Chapter Nine

Only On the Web

Acrobat Reader

MUST HAVES

http://www.adobe.com/

Adobe invented the Portable Document Format
(pdf) file system, which is a way of delivering text
and image documents such as manuals and
information sheets, in a form that the reader cannot
edit or alter. Many downloadable documents now
come as pdfs rather than Word or HTML
documents. The Acrobat Reader is free. Get Version
3.0 or higher, and the site allows you to specify a
nearby host for faster access.

Internet tip

Command-line switches for Internet Explorer – Internet Explorer 4.0 and above accepts command-line switches. Start, Run iexplore.exe and add one of the following switches: -channelband (Launch IE as a Desktop Toolbar, showing the Channels Directory of the current user – only works when Active Desktop is off); -e (Launch IE in Explorer mode); -k (Launch IE in Kiosk mode); -new (Launch IE in a new process); -nohome (Launch IE but ignore the Homepage setting); -slf (Launch IE and connect to default home page from cache).

Advice For HTML Authors   WEB AUTHORING

http://ugweb.cs.ualberta.ca/~gerald/guild/style.html

The HTML Writers Guild offers sound advice for web designers, and provides links to other useful tools and resources.

Alexa

SEARCH ENGINES

http://www.filez.com/alexa.html

Alexa is not a search engine but a free navigation service which adds context to content. It works with your existing browser and has features such as: information on who is behind your favourite web site, site ratings, recommended links to related sites, archiving (so that if a page or web site is no longer available, Alexa may find a copy eliminating the dreaded '404 Not Found'), the chance to write your own review, reference tools from Encyclopaedia Britannica Online and Merriam-Webster's Dictionary and Thesaurus.

Alli's Backgrounds

BACKGROUNDS, IMAGES AND ANIMATIONS

http://www.tecinfo.com/~alli/ani/bkgrnd.htm

Tiling backgrounds, textures, desktop wallpaper and everything you need are collected and categorised on this nice, simple site. Lovely muzak in the background, too.

Internet tip

Index = default – HTTP assumes that the default file in a web site is called index.htm or default.htm (or .html). So typing http://thingy/dir/ will actually take you to http://thingy/dir/index.htm. It is possible for a web site designer to designate a different file as the default file (eg start.htm) in which case, you will start at that page.

Art Today BACKGROUNDS, IMAGES AND ANIMATIONS

http://www.arttoday.com/PD-0025000/

Art Today is one of the best-designed sites in this category, as you might expect, but rarely get, from an online art site. It has good quality clipart, buttons, arrows, bullets, graphics, backgrounds, rules, textures, icons, photos and animated gifs. This site offers 40,000 images free if you subscribe (fee) and 250,000 if you pay an annual subscription of around £20.

Ask Jeeves   SEARCH ENGINES

http://www.askjeeves.com/

Saving the best until last, meet Jeeves. This is
nothing short of a miracle. You can genuinely ask
Jeeves a question like 'Why is grass green?' or 'Why
do I never see baby pigeons?' and get a sensible
answer, or at least a good place to find out.
Compare this with the human-based Allexperts.com
(http://www.allexperts.com/).

Amnesty International   NEWS

http://www.amnesty.org/

This is a huge site, making use of Amnesty's archives
on human rights issues worldwide, background
material, annual reports, press releases back to 1995
and a wealth of links. The front page carries
bulletins on the latest human rights concerns.

Internet tip

Internet Explorer text dump – If you think Internet Explorer has loaded a page but it's not showing it, press the down arrow and the text will be dumped onto the screen.

BBC News   NEWS

http://news.bbc.co.uk/

As might be expected from the world's premier news organisation, this site is up to date, well-organised and good-looking. It also links to channel information and the home page of your favourite TV programme.

Browser Plug-Ins   MUST HAVES

http://home.netscape.com/plugins/index.html

Plug-ins are small programs which help your browser play audio, video and other files. This is the best place to find plug-ins for Navigator/ Communicator and also ActiveX controls, which perform the same function within Internet Explorer.

Clipart Castle's Animated Gif Fantasy
BACKGROUNDS, IMAGES AND ANIMATIONS

http://www.clipartcastle.com/jokers/animatedgifs.htm

Anyone who needs fantasy-themed gifs for
Dungeons and Dragons sites and so on will find
just about everything they need here. A nice touch
is the castle theme on the site itself, which will
make it attractive to Doom gamers and fantasy fans.

Completely Free Software   SOFTWARE

http://www.completelyfreesoftware.com/

Just what it says, CFS is nicely organised with a
good index, a New Software section, excellent
search facilities and a special section for web
authors. A great feature is a £10 (roughly) CD-ROM
of software shipped free anywhere in the world.

Composing Good HTML   WEB AUTHORING

http://www.cs.cmu.edu/~tilt/cgh/

This is a useful guide to a number of the more
important issues in design of web pages.

Internet tip

Microsoft Exchange and Microsoft Network – Often, Exchange users find their system tries to log into Microsoft Network (MSN) when they don't want it to – on an intranet, for instance. Set up a separate profile for Exchange without the MSN drivers. Open Control Panel, Mail & Fax, create a new profile and only add Internet Mail to it. Change Exchange to prompt you for the profile to use when starting.

Dave Central   SOFTWARE

http://www.davecentral.com/

Quirky, idiosyncratic and clearly one man's labour of love, Dave will keep you up to date on the latest shareware and freeware software for downloading. An interesting recent addition is a What's New ticker-tape – a small Java applet which displays everything added to the database that day. Dave also has domain name registration, a newsletter and links to providers' home pages.

Windows tip

Close a window but save size and position – Hold down Ctrl while closing and the size and place of the window will be saved.

Driverguide.Com   COMPUTING AND INTERNET

http://www.driverguide.com/

There are few things more frustrating than not having the right driver for your new printer, scanner, sound card, etc. This guide to finding drivers on the internet has them all, nicely structured and usually with installation instructions. Registration is required.

Drudge Report   NEWS

http://www.drudgereport.com/

The gutter press at its best, and on the web. Poor design, but infuriatingly captivating content.

Internet tip

Search for a URL – You can search for a URL with a browser by typing url: in the Search box before the URL itself (or part of it). For instance, url:http://www.fifeweb would find any site with this string in it. This is useful for finding whether a search engine has a particular site in its database (after you have submitted it, for example) or whether any other sites link to that URL.

e-Zineseek   BULLETIN BOARDS

http://www.ezineseek.com/forum/index.cgi

There are simply too many electronic magazines (e-zines) in too many categories and catering for too diverse a range of specialist interests to make any sensible choice as to quality. It is almost impossible to keep up with the e-zines and bulletin boards which could offer you an opportunity to publicise yourself or your business. Fortunately, this site does a lot of the hard work for you.

Internet tip

Organise Internet Explorer –
Click on Favorites, Organise
and you can move folders
about, create new ones,
rename existing folders,
shift shortcuts between
them or delete them
altogether. You don't have
to live with the options
Microsoft gave you.

FAQ Finder

COMPUTING AND INTERNET

http://ps.superb.net/FAQ/

This site allows the surfer to search for Frequently
Asked Questions by name or category from about
1,800 FAQs.

Filez

SOFTWARE

http://www.filez.com

Filez looks good (apart from the irritating tendency,
adopted from the hacking fraternity, of ending all
plurals with a 'z') and loads fast with a claimed 75
million files to search! It also has useful Top 20 and
What's New listings, plus the offer of a CD software
collection.

Internet tip

Restore a missing plug-in or file – If Internet Explorer 4 has a missing plug-in or corrupted file, Start, Run | c:\windows\system\msiexec .exe /f. Other switches are /a (network installation), /i (install) and /x (uninstall).

InfoJump   NEWS

http://www.InfoJump.com/

InfoJump is a great resource for finding past and current articles from over 3,500 magazines, newspapers, journals, newsletters and e-zines. As such, InfoJump makes a superb research tool. Whatever you want to write, rest assured somebody has writen it first, and it's probably here somewhere.

Mars Exploration   VRML

http://mpfwww.jpl.nasa.gov/

NASA's Jet Propulsion Lab (JPL) has chronicled its microrover landing on Mars. Using VRML, anyone can explore the Mars surface from this web site. See also **http://www.bchip.com/mars/nav.html**.

Modem and comms tip

Redialling with Dial-Up Networking – Why isn't there a redial feature for those times when you get an engaged signal? Well, there is, but it's fairly well hidden. Open My Computer, Dial-up Networking, Connections, Settings, tick the Redial box and set the Retries and Wait time parameters.

Net Use

DIRECTORIES

http://www.bgsu.edu/departments/tcom/users.html

Dr Bruce Klopfenstein of Bowling Green University produced this comprehensive page of links to web user research. It contains every sort of web traffic analysis, some of it historical and therefore out of date, but still useful when planning an assault on the wired world.

Modem and comms tip

Get a faster connection to your ISP – Open Dial-Up Networking, select the connection you use, right-click, select Properties and in Server Types tab, untick Log On to Network. Verify that you can still connect. Most Internet Service Providers (ISPs) do not use this setting, and it can take up to one minute to time-out. If you can't connect, tick it again.

Newshub

NEWS

http://www.newshub.com/

A real hoover of a site, NewsHub integrates and reports headlines from the world's main news sources every 15 minutes, and each section carries a tally as to how many new stories have been recently added. Therefore all stories are current. Some of it, however, is no more than press releases. Do the sources pay for this? What is clever is the fact that NewsHub is fully automated, using intelligent agent technology.

Internet tip

Do it on your holidays – To connect to the web and download updated pages even when you're away, open Favorites, Subscriptions, Options, Global Subscription Properties (or by clicking the Subscriptions icon in the System Tray), click Dial Up and tick Yes, connect to the Internet automatically. Select which dial-up to use, add any username and password required, select Daily Schedule and Weekly Schedule to enter your choices. Or take the default, daily between midnight and 5 a.m.

New Scientist

NEWS

http://www.newscientist.com

Among the first of the mainstream magazines to take the web seriously, New Scientist also provides content additional to that available in its paper pages. Two great features are Instant Genius (boiled-down all-you-need-to-know summaries of, say, quantum mechanics) and Last Word with answers to all those questions like: Why is the sky blue? and How do skateboarders jump their skateboards?

Modem and comms tip

Dial your computer – Away from the office or home? Dial-up networking can bring them to you. Click on Start, Programs, Accessories, Communications, Dial-Up Networking to set up a new dial-up client. The computer you are dialling in to must be set up as a network server and have shared resources. Both your computer and the network server must have modems installed.

Obscure News Store   NEWS

http://www.obscurestore.com/

The strangest news from all corners of the world makes strangely compulsive reading.

Quicktime   MUST HAVES

http://www.apple.com/quicktime/download/index.html

With Quicktime 4, all that lovely streaming video, sound, music, 3-D and virtual reality can be yours. Remember to choose the PC or Mac version.

Research It

http://www.itools.com/research-it/

This site takes a different tack and assumes that sometimes what you want is not a web site link, but an answer. Organised very nicely into six broad categories, this site takes you directly, by keyword, to useful research tools such as dictionaries, translators, maps and phone books. Check out the CIA's World Factbook. They don't know Scotland exists, which is fine by me. But did you know that in 1998 the UK had 12,069,296 males fit for military service? The CIA did. Spooky!

Shockwave

MUST HAVES

http://www.macromedia.com/shockwave/download/

This is the best place to get Shockwave and Flash programs. Many web designers use Macromedia's Shockwave and Flash to deliver multimedia. The add-ons needed to play such files are available free. Make sure you get the correct versions for your browser. After downloading and installing, return to this site and check out the 'Shocked Site of the Day'.

Internet tip

URL shortcuts – You can create internet shortcuts manually with Notepad. Open it and type two lines: [InternetShortcut] (then on a new line)

URL=http://www.burble.com/index.html (or another URL). Save the file on your desktop as 'Link to BURBLE' or whatever. Click on it to be connected.

Softseek   SOFTWARE

http://www.softseek.com

This may well be the best place to check out and download the latest software. Dated look, but well organised into a hierarchy of meaningful categories. Features include New Releases, Top Downloads, Editors' Picks and a good search engine. A minor gripe is that it doesn't show file sizes, so it's not immediately obvious whether it's worth looking at the description of a 40MB file you're never going to download. It does say whether the download is shareware, freeware, a timed trial or a demo. Newsletter sign-up available. Links to providers' home pages.

Modem and comms tip

Modem set up trouble – Don't overlook the importance of ports – for a Direct-Cable Connection a parallel port is faster (it sends data 8 bits at a time) than even the fastest serial port (1 bit at a time)

Tim Berners-Lee Style Guide for Online Hypertext   WEB AUTHORING

http://www.w3.org/hypertext/WWW/Provider/Style/Overview.html

For the authoritative word on HTML, who better than the man largely responsible for the web? This is essential reading for anyone serious about web design.

Internet tip

Subscribe! – The Work Offline feature functions best in conjunction with Subscriptions, one of Internet Explorer 4 and 5's most powerful features. By subscribing to sites, you can download changes to your favourite pages and view them whenever you like – even when you're not connected. Subscribing is a good way to do all your downloading at once, at a convenient time, such as while you're asleep.

Transparent and Interlaced Gifs   WEB DESIGN

http://www.nctweb.com/nct/software/transgif.html

GIF files can be confusing. The basic rule is not to mix non-transparent and interlaced GIFs, but there is more to it than that. This tutorial addresses the differences between transparent and other GIF files and deals with interlacing.

Tucows

SOFTWARE

http://www.tucows.com/

The Ultimate Collection of Winsock Software has
expanded from just Winsock utilities since it was
launched in 1992, but the name – and the obvious
but appealing two cows logo – have stayed. The
farmyard theme continues with Head of the Herd
(editor's choice software) and eBarn Store. The best
feature is the wide availability of mirror sites –
despite what anyone says, geography does matter on
the internet and the closer a server is to you, the
faster your downloads.

Modem and comms tip

***Check which serial port
your modem is on*** – Open
Control Panel, System,
Device Manager, click on
the + beside Modem, select
the modem you use, click

Properties, Modem and see
what it says under Port. You
can also change the
Speaker Volume for the
Modem dial tone if you like.

Virtual Library   DIRECTORIES

http://celtic.stanford.edu/vlib/Overview.html

As befits a major seat of learning, Stanford
University has put together a good library of sites in
roughly the same categories as Yahoo. To save your
browsing time, there are mirror sites in various
locations, including the UK. It is simply a list of
links (access to about 300 other Virtual Libraries).
But it is cleverly structured with alphabetical listing
and a keyword search, plus the ability to add your
own or favourite Vitrual Library, subject to their
approval. This is what local branch libraries are up
against unless they embrace the concept.

Browser tip

See image details – Want to view an image on its own? Right–click on the image and choose View Image. Want to know the filename and location of an image? Right–click and choose Copy Image Location. Paste it to an open Notepad window.

Webring

DIRECTORIES

http://www.webring.org

Clearly not designed by a librarian (in that it actually has a good design), the webring gives access to hundreds of thousands of member web sites organised by interest groupings called 'rings'. It isn't selective as anyone can apply to join a ring or create a new one of at least five sites. However, they will deny service or suspend a ring if the system is being 'abused'. The directory is called – wouldn't you know it – Ringworld, doubtless managed by Ringmasters. Webring has 500,000 daily visitors and 500,000 member sites in 40,000 Rings.

Internet tip

MetaSearch Engines – Sometimes a single search engine can't find the information you want, but a MetaSearcher will interrogate a number of engines for you. Start with Dogpile (http://www.dogpile.com/) or MetaFind (http://www.metafind.com/).

WinZip

MUST HAVES

http://www.winzip.com

A lot of your downloads will be zipped (compressed) files and WinZip is the best way to unzip them. Get WinZip 7 and remember to pay for it later!

Internet tip

Internet dial-up shortcut – Start browsing right from start-up. Install MS Plus! (uninstall Exchange first) or Internet Explorer and run the Internet setup wizard. Select 'AutoDial' in your DUN connection to your Internet Service Provider. To look at a URL click Start, Run and type the URL (http://whatever.co.uk/file.htm) in the box. Win 95 and 98 will start Internet Explorer, connect and find the site.

A Selection of Newsgroups to get you started   NEWSGROUPS

Getting into newsgroups is rather like going to a cocktail party for 100 million guests. The trick is to find the groups that happen to be talking about things that interest you, then moving between them as the evening progresses. Unlike a party, however, internet newsgroups are organised logically and can be tracked down by their names. There are well over 25,000 newsgroups, but ranked hierarchically from starting points. These are the 10 main ones:

alt (alternative) – weirdness and a lot of 'adult' material, not for the prim;

Internet tip

Trace slow connections – Frustrated by slow connections and failures? Windows 95 and 98 have a diagnostic tool – a DOS program called tracert.exe which follows the link between your computer and any other one on the internet. It tells you how many hops you made before your ultimate destination, whether each jump connected and how long it took. Open a DOS box with Start, Programs, MS-DOS Prompt and type tracert.exe www.whatsitcalled.com.(or any other URL). Note the missing 'http://'. Type EXIT to close the DOS box.

biz (business) – commercial newsgroups, where advertising is allowed;

comp (computing) – the one for the tekkies and anoraks amongst us, with endless discussions on the relative merits of printer driver version 1.1.1.1 vs 1.1.1.0a, for instance;

news – this covers the business of newsgroups itself;

rec (recreation) – which includes sports and so on;

talk – discussion for the sake of it and a haven for insomniacs;

Browser tip

Print to the right paper size – Some web pages (especially US ones) are designed to print on 8½′ x 11′ paper. If it is a large image and you want it all on one page, save it to your hard drive (right-click and 'Save As...') and use a graphics program to reduce it to fit.

sci (science) – a good place to have real discussions with real scientists, the online equivalent of the scientific conference;

soc – society, culture etc;

uk – many countries have their own newsgroup hierarchy for topics of local interest (de for Germany, for instance);

misc (miscellaneous) – anything which doesn't fit anywhere else, which is hard to believe.

Below these categories the sites are named logically but in an ever-expanding tree of subdivisions separated by dots. Some examples –

• alt.alien.vampire.flonk.flonk.flonk. Oh, come now!

Internet tip

Use Netscape to upload via FTP – Connect to an ftp server using the command: ftp://username:password@ftp.hostname.com/directory_name/. If you prefer not to type your password directly in the Location window, leave it out and Netscape will prompt you for it when it connects. Once connected, click and drag files from Windows Explorer into the Netscape window to upload them to the ftp server.

- biz.marketplace.services.discussion – a guide to transactions in the misc.forsale. and biz.marketplace.newsgroups, with suggestions for many other advertising groups –
- comp.sys.hp.hardware – everything you want to know about Hewlett Packard
- hardware.news.announce.newusers – a good place to start, lots of information for new users
- rec.aquaria.freshwater.plants – just what it says.
- sci.med.prostate.prostatitis – including the answer to the burning question 'Is there some way to make bike riding less painful?'
- soc.genealogy.surnames – starting point for discussions on name origins.

Modem and comms tip

Dial-up troubleshooting with a phone – Check your Dial-Up Networking setup without a phone. A relatively easy way is by establishing a Direct-Cable Connection between a laptop and a desktop PC before you try anything else. If it works, all your passwords are all correct – often a stumbling block – and it hasn't cost you a phone call.

- talk.bizarre – honestly, what some people do with their spare time.
- uk.media.tv.sf.x-files – local fandom for the FBI Sci-Fi.
- misc.writing.screenplays – instead of hanging around in Hollywood soda shops, aspiring screenwriters meet here.

Chapter Ten

Fun and Games

Aloud.Com

THEATRE

http://www.aloud.com/

This UK-based Online Ticket Service, Event Guide and Venue Directory is exactly what it says – buy a ticket for just about anything, just about anywhere. Really.

Animal Aid Online

PETS

http://www.animalaid.org.uk/

This animal rights campaign site deals with anti-vivisection, animal experimentation, factory farming and vegetarianism. Well-organised and easy to navigate with a good education section, it makes up in enthusiasm what it lacks in balance.

Start-up tip

Warm restart – A warm restart is where the PC doesn't switch off (as opposed to a cold restart, where it does). Click on

Start, Shutdown, check restart and hold down the shift when you click OK.

Answering Machine

THEATRE

http://www.answeringmachine.co.uk/

Now here is a truly valuable service – the web's largest collection of celebrity voice answering machine messages from Arnold Schwarzenegger to Homer Simpson, all downloadable for your amusement.

Are You A Nerd?

SURREAL

http://www.frontiernet.net/~jbennett/nerd/n500test.html

Find out with this 500-question test. And anyone willing to answer 500 questions online probably is.

Avoiding Genealogical Grief

GENEALOGY, HERALDRY AND ANCESTORS

http://www.rootsweb.com/roots-l/20ways.html

This list of twenty suggestions is good basic help for beginners to genealogical research.

Bad Art

ALTERNATIVE ARTS

http://www.badart.com/

Good bad art is always powerful. And so is a nearby sewage farm. Vito Salvatore scoured America for the most appallingly bad art he could find, and succeeded. The resulting site is a testament to the complete lack of talent out there.

BBC Online

TV AND FILM

http://www.bbc.co.uk/

This is a truly integrated site, which goes beyond listings to include news, weather, education and everything you would expect from Auntie, including a Jobs List with online application forms for all aspiring media moguls.

Start-up tip

Start up in DOS – Use 'Command Prompt Only' during start up. Holding down the F8 key while Win 95 or 98 starts gives a menu of boot options, one of which is Command Prompt Only. If you find your system still boots into Windows, open the AUTOEXEC.BAT file (with Notepad or sysedit.exe) and check there isn't a command in it that starts Windows such as win. Remove the line or, better still, type REM at the beginning of the line.

BBC Top Gear   CARS

http://www.topgear.beeb.com/

In another of the BBC's excellent TV-to-magazine-to-web exercises, Jeremy Clarkson and his chums get to drive the hairiest cars and bikes and enthuse about them. Apart from excellent and relevant links, the site has a daily news section, a carchase feature and fantasy Formula 1.

Bitter Waitress   SURREAL

http://www.bitterwaitress.com/

The next time you get a particularly good one off at the staff in a restaurant, better check to see if you get listed here. Waiters swap advice on unwelcome patrons and difficult customers. The Celebrity Role of Dishonour may stimulate some over-the-top tipping in the near future.

Blazon   GENEALOGY, HERALDRY AND ANCESTORS

http://www.platypus.clara.co.uk/blazon.htm

Blazon is a good heraldry shareware program, very useful for producing quick visualisations of existing or new designs, and good for the beginner to heraldry.

Body Magic   SURREAL

http://www.eventmediagroup.com/bodymagic/

Contortionists abound in this site dedicated to the noble art of getting your leg round behind your ears. Stunning pictures.

Start-up tip

Power Management – Your PC probably has some sort of Advanced Power Management function, probably in Control Panel. Set this to switch off the hard drive after a decent interval (30 minutes, say) and set the monitor to go on Standby (NOT 'off') after 15 or so. A nudge of the mouse should set it springing back to life. Do not set a password you will inevitably forget. Some monitors don't take well to power-offs and won't come on again, in which case disable the monitor Standby Option.

Bowienet

MUSIC

http://www.davidbowie.com/

You would trust Bowie to produce a really good online community for the fans, wouldn't you? Apart from the stunning design and the predictable shopping opportunity, there is a good selection of Bowie art, advance album downloads and Ziggy's own virtual world.

CD Now   MUSIC

http://www.cdnow.com/

This is the aural equivalent of Amazon. Be careful
of incurring import tax and VAT. It also has reviews,
sound clips and a personalise feature so that you
can browse for the music it knows you like.

Centre for the Easily
Amused   JUST PLAIN WEIRD

http://www.amused.com/

There are a lot of strange sites in here, but the
webcam links to grass growing and paint peeling
take the biscuit.

Classic Motor Online   CARS

http://www.classicmotor.co.uk

Those of us who drive Classic cars need to know
about events, rallies, auctions, spares, services and
the occasional kind shoulder to cry on. This is also
a good place to buy and sell vintage cars.

Start-up tip

Shut down – Aaargh! Too soon! – If you start to shut down and suddenly realise you should have done something else, wait for the 'It is now safe for you to shut down your computer' message and type win followed by pressing Enter. (This may not work if you have an ATX-format PC which switches off automatically at the message.)

Cupid's Network

SINGLES AND DATING

http://www.cupidnet.com/

This site brings together USA sites, International sites (an extensive list of over 400 links and which includes Russian Romance/Marriage Tours and the wonderfully named SingleJew.com), Phone and Chat Lines, Singles Events (in America), Religious Sites, Singles Travel, Singles Literature and a Bookstore. Apparently I'm compatible with three women in Alabama who'd love to meet me. Plane fare?

Start-up tip

Start up with no logo – If the Windows logo annoys you to death, search for the file msdos.sys, with Start, Find, open it with Notepad.exe, find the [Options] section and add the line 'Logo='. Then save, close and reboot.

Cyberdrive   CARS

http://www.cyberdrive.co.uk/index.html

Driving test coming up soon? The Virtual Driving Theory Test might help. The Stationery Office (formerly HMSO and publishers of the Highway Code) and the Driving Standards Agency have collaborated on this site which allows you to improve your knowledge before taking the actual Theory Test. Alternatively, take a test right away using your credit card. There is a database of over 600 questions, five Theory Test papers and an index of TSO publications to order to help you pass.

Start-up tip

Disable floppy disc scan – Fed up waiting while Windows checks for a floppy every time you start up? Right-click on My Computer, Properties, Performance, File System, Floppy disk and untick Search for new floppy... followed by OK. Close any open windows. If the File System Properties window doesn't have a Floppy Disc tab, you don't have a problem, do you?

Datemaker   SINGLES AND DATING

http://www.datemaker.co.uk/

Now this is a really clever site that makes excellent if rather cheeky use of the web's database integration possibilities. If you searched for, say, singles OR dating OR introduction AND Berkshire you would get a page which would simply take you (always) to the home page. An example would be 'Click here for Love in Co Fermanagh' which seems like a reasonable request. Once you register you receive an ID, etc. plus the chance to answer 60 questions and some essays (do it offline).

Explorer tip

System information from Windows Explorer – Access your system information from Windows Explorer, without opening the Control Panel. Right-click My Computer, Properties to open System Properties.

Right-click Network Neighborhood to open Network Properties. Make shortcuts to the other Control Panel applets by dragging them from the Control Panel window onto the desktop.

The Edge   CHAT ROOMS

http://www.edge.org/

Big brains debate big issues. This is mind-expanding Radio 4-type stuff and a proper use of discussion forums – I mean, you won't get the likes of Esther Dyson, Stephen Jay Gould and Richard Dawkins descending to the usual cyber-chat level of Anyone there? {:{ Mike here (:~}> Hi Mike ?. Send your feedback to the Reality Club and help decide the most important invention of the last two millennia. I propose the electric toaster.

Start-up tip

Make a boot disk – A Startup or Boot disk is useful if you have hard disc problems, or want a 'clean boot'. Click Start, Settings, | Control Panel, double-click Add/Remove Programs, click Startup Disk, Create Disk.

Field Museum of Natural History   VIRTUAL MUSEUMS AND GALLERIES

http://www.fmnh.org./

The Field Museum of Natural History, Chicago, is a good example of making the best use of new web technology. Check out the running Triceratops!

Film.Com   TV AND FILM

http://www.film.com/

This excellent and comprehensive web site for film buffs offers news, stories, reviews and film clips, plus the chance to buy movie memorabilia. Short films playable on your PC require the latest RealPlayer G2 software, downloadable free.

Film Finder

TV AND FILM

`http://www.yell.co.uk/yell/ff/home.html`

What's on at the flicks? Here's the place to find out.
It genuinely had the latest information on films
showing in my small town. Plus info on the films
and the phone no. of the cinema so I could check.
This site is an alliance of *Yellow Pages* and the Press
Association, so should be as comprehensive as it is.
Then it listed the restaurant/pub/taxi near to the
cinema by using a *Yellow Page* search (one of each
category my personal favourites). It works!

Fine Arts Museums of San Francisco

VIRTUAL MUSEUMS AND GALLERIES

`http://www.island.com/famsf/famsf_welcome.html`

One of the best, and a good example
of elegant migration from 'real'
to 'virtual'.

Explorer tip

Complete delete – Normally, deleting files actually stores them in the Recycle bin, in case they have to be retrieved later. To delete immediately, either hold down Shift while dragging items to Recycle or select a file and press Shift + Delete.

Flypower

JUST PLAIN WEIRD

http://www.flypower.com

This site is all about paper airplanes powered by house flies. There are regular Tech Updates on new research and development projects and an 'Alternate Engines Page'. Bzzz. Excellent design and graphics by people of real, if misguided, talent.

Gamesdomain

GAMES

http://www.gamesdomain.co.uk/

We all get stuck sometimes, and a cheats site is a great help. This massive site's archive also has games news, free stuff, downloads and online favourites.

Gamespot

GAMES

http://www.gamespot.com/

This is a truly comprehensive site for game fanatics. Good for downloads of demos, it also has news, reviews, previews, hints, features, designer diaries, columns, letters, a beta-test version centre, contests and a release calendar. Nicely designed and fast loading, a particularly good feature is the 3-D model gallery, in which are the tools to grab a character, creature or weapon from your favourite game and manipulate it.

Gardenworld

GARDENING

http://www.gardenworld.co.uk/

UK garden centres, plant suppliers, garden product manufacturers, events, new product reviews, books, competitions, diary, gardening questions and answers – what more do you need?

Web tip

Search engines matter –
Almost all of your traffic will come from a few search engines. A top 10 ranking in a major search engine like AltaVista, Lycos, or Infoseek will generate far more hits than an expensive banner ad. Over 95% of the search engine traffic to most web sites comes from the 15 major search engines.

Genhome   GENEALOGY, HERALDRY AND ANCESTORS

http://www.genhomepage.com/full.html

This is a huge collection of links to genealogical guides, maps, software, societies and newsgroups.

Start-up tip

Boot up in a Windows DOS session – If you prefer Windows 95 or 98 to boot up in an MS-DOS session, do this: open msdos.sys in MS-DOS Editor or with Notepad Find the line 'BootGUI=1' and change it to 'BootGUI=0' – if your MSDOS.sys file doesn't have 'BootGUI=1' add the line 'BootGUI=0' near the top of the file. Save, close and restart your PC to enter an MS-DOS session. The MS-DOS Editor is involved at the DOS command prompt (c:\>) by typing Edit (in this case, edit msdos.sys).

Handbag

CHAT ROOMS

http://www.handbag.com/

Just what the world needs – a women's gossip site. Boots think so, hence the Powder Room, plus discussion groups and chat areas on health issues, links to job sites and entertainment pointers. Ooooh, Mavis.

Explorer tip

File names and extensions – The MS-DOS name must conform to the '8.3' rule (abcdefgh.123) but Windows has no limit on extensions (ABCDEFGH.123456), file name length (abcdefghabcdefghabcdefgh.123) or a combination of these (12345678901234567890123456789012345678901234567890.abcdef). Long names with capitals, spaces, underscores and hyphens are allowed (e.g. This is my Document-duplicate_2.worddoc).

Heroic Stories   SURREAL

http://www.heroicstories.com/

Randy Cassingham has published This is True, one of the largest free subscription newsletters on the internet, weekly since 1994. It reports bizarre-but-true stories and headlines from the world's press. This new venture intends to publicise good things that people do, which may not make it into the newspapers, such as *How Mr Sulu Talked Me Out Of Smoking*. One to watch, definitely.

Explorer tip

Undo File Move or File Rename – If you accidentally rename or move a file (or forget where you just moved a file to), in Windows Explorer, click Edit, Undo or press CTRL+Z.

Internet Gaming Zone   GAMES

http://www.zone.com/

This zone has free membership, unlike some.

IUMA   MUSIC

http://www.iuma.com/IUMA/index_graphic.html

The Internet Underground Music Archive claims to feature the music of over 3,000 independent musicians. The retro-50s design is appealing. For those with a slow connection there is a cut-down version (IUMA-Lite). There is training on how to manipulate downloadable and streaming sound for the web, with a CD-ROM of software utilities and song samples, an online music store and a 'radio station' for online broadcasting of 100 songs while you surf.

Explorer tip

File names and extensions –
If you want to use long file
names in a DOS box or an
older Windows versions
(pre-Windows 95) – there
are often good reasons for
this, for instance, if the
program folder is called 'My

Program Folder' or
something similar – put the
file or folder name in
quotes, e.g. to change to a
'long name' folder like My
Documents, type cd 'My
Documents'.

Kissthisguy.Com   JUST PLAIN WEIRD

http://www.kissthisguy.com/index.html

Ever misheard a song then sang it on a bus?
Embarrassing. This site is dedicated to all of us who
thought Sting was singing 'I'm a lethal idiot'. There
is a huge collection of wrong songs (and the right
versions) including the famous Hendrix misquote
used in the site title. Clever use of frames and
databases make this site a joy to browse.

Latter Day Saints

GENEALOGY, HERALDRY AND ANCESTORS

http://www.familysearch.org/

If anybody is going to get genealogy right, it will be the Church of Jesus Christ of the Latter Day Saints. The Mormons believe that the dead can be saved retrospectively by claiming them as ancestors, so family histories are crucial. To this end, they have done heroic work around the world preserving, collecting, annotating and gathering together a vast array of genealogical and public records. Previously, it was necessary to visit one of their Centres. Now, at last, these resources are online with 300 million names. Simple name searches will access a variety of databases for family histories and pedigrees, including near misses, for surname variants. They all deserve sainthood, just for undertaking this mammoth, never-ending (in this life) task. The related Utah Valley Library site (**http://www.lib.byu.edu/dept/uvrfhc/**) has additional resources as does FAMILYSEARCH (**http://www.lib.byu.edu/~uvrfhc/famsrch.html**).

Explorer tip

Drag and drop with right-click – In Windows Explorer you can drag a file or object to another folder with the left mouse button, but use the right mouse button and you will get a useful set of options such as Move here, Copy here or Create Shortcut(s) here.

Lorryspotting   SURREAL

http://www.lorryspotting.com/

More people indulge in the gentle art of spotting the Eddie Stobart heavy goods fleet than go to Church on a Sunday, allegedly. So here's the latest info, lorry photos, a chat room and haulage news. Keep on truckin', Eddie.

MCN List   VIRTUAL MUSEUMS AND GALLERIES

http://world.std.com/~mcn

The Museum Computer Network maintains a hotlist of over 500 museums on the web.

Explorer tip

Two directory views – There are those of us who mourn the passing of Windows 3.1 File Manager, not least for its ability to show two or more Directories (Folders) at once. To get the same effect with Windows Explorer, open it twice and have different Folders in each. Right-click the Windows Task Bar and choose to tile vertically or horizontally. You can drag files and folders between them. This is especially helpful if another computer is mapped as a network drive. It makes moving and copying much easier.

Midi Web Resources   AUDIO

http://midibiz.w1.com/websites/websoft.htm

Windows come with a restricted range of playable MIDI tunes. Here, there are various downloadable midi programs for music writing and replaying with descriptions of their functions, plus sound samples.

Start-up tip

Customise start up and Exit screens – The Windows logo screen at start up and the message at shutdown are simple bitmap graphics in the Windows folder called, respectively, logow.sys and logos.sys, or something very similar. They can be altered with any graphics program. Replace the standard 'It is now safe for you to shut down your computer' message on friends' machines with a far more alarming message, or an upside-down graphic. A colleague used this ploy to prove that the expensive computer consultants hired by her firm didn't know the real basics – they got fired, she got a formal reprimand and a promotion. This is in no way a recommendation!

MTV

TV AND FILM

http://www.mtv.com/

Anyone into popular music will want to access this online magazine from the premier TV music channel. Apart from the obvious listings and MTV-related news, this site also has a useful alphabetical list of bands. Only the latest and greatest are there – no Beatles, for example! Mind you, ZZ Top made it.

Explorer tip

Open a file with a chosen application – Want to open a file, but not with the associated application? If you have associated a file type with an application, clicking on the file will open it using that application. For instance, clicking a file with a .htm extension usually opens it in a browser, but you may want to open it in a text editor such as Notepad. You can bypass this by holding SHIFT and right-clicking the file, then click Open With to choose the program you want to use. Ticking the Always Use option re-associates the file type.

The National Anxiety Center   SURREAL

http://www.anxietycenter.com/

The Good News is that the Bad News is wrong! The Earth is fine, there is no global warming, America has 28% more standing timber than in 1952, the world has infinite capacity to deal with garbage and crime rates continue to decline. Now, isn't that nice?

Explorer tip

Move a multiple file selection – In Windows Explorer, select a file, then hold down Shift while clicking another file. This selects all the files between and including those two. If the files you want to select are not all together, hold down Ctrl while clicking on the ones you want to select. They can then all be dragged, deleted, etc. together.

Palaeolithic Painted Cave

VIRTUAL MUSEUMS AND GALLERIES

http://www.culture.fr/culture/arcnat/chauvet/en/

Brilliant images and excellent text from the recently discovered cave at Vallon – Pont-d'Arc. Apart from this 'virtual museum' the caves are 'off limits' to protect the fragile cave paintings, so this is the best opportunity to see them.

Web tip

Links increase web traffic – A higher percentage of web traffic comes from links than even search engines. And since some search engines rate a given site according to how many other sites link to it, this can help your rankings. Swap links with other sites, or submit your site to one of the many links lists like http://urlomatic.azzsol.com

Pets Corner

PETS

http://www.catholic.org.uk/Kidz_Stuff/under_13/
Pets_Corner/default.htm

This is a good site for kids (organised by age ranges) on the care and feeding of pets. A real vet answers questions.

Policescanner

AUDIO

http://www.policescanner.com/

Frighten your loved ones – tune into NYPD, LAPD, fire department broadcasts and live conversations between air traffic control and airline pilots. Scary. Requires RealPlayer, downloadable free.

Web tip

Fast browsing – You can Edit, Paste a URL in location box and hit return to browse to it.

Popcorn

TV AND FILM

http://www.popcorn.co.uk/

This good-looking site for the rabid cinema buff has news on the latest releases, celebrity gossip, listings and interviews with the stars of the silver screen. 'Allegedly' is a section devoted to which celebrity is doing what to whom.

Royal Horticultural Society

GARDENING

http://www.rhs.org.uk/

The RHS is the Guv'nor, after all. And they do themselves justice with this superbly designed site. Apart from the fantastically informative Plant Finder (and where to get over 70,000 species) it has details of RHS-run gardens, courses, events and more.

Explorer tip

Reorder your files – In an Explorer Window (Details View) there are tabs at the top which will arrange files and folders by size, type, date modified, etc. Clicking on these more than once toggles the sort order from ascending to descending and back again. This is useful, say, for finding the largest or most recent file in a folder. To get the details view, click View, Details.

Soundresource.net   AUDIO

http://www.soundresource.net/

This is one of the largest WAV and MP3 archives on the web – over 2,000 sound clips from films, cartoons and television shows as well as other media. This is the place to get Homer Simpson saying 32 Dohs in 15 seconds. Right click to Save to your disk, remembering to respect others' copyright!

Explorer tip

Refresh your desktop or Windows Explorer view – F5 is a general command for refreshing whichever view you are in. This is useful if you have deleted or moved files or desktop icons.

Spinner   AUDIO

http://www.spinner.com/

Come the day of free internet phone calls, this will be my only radio and I'll throw away my CD player – over 100 channels of music back-to-back with details of the track playing.

Sporting Life   SPORTS

http://www.sporting-life.com/

This site is the best for full-time scores and reports, form guides, instant results and up-to-the-minute news.

Web tip

Resumable downloads – There is nothing more frustrating than getting 95% of a one-hour download, then the phone cuts off. Or finding that the end has truncated. Ask your ISP if their server supports resumable downloads. If so, the user can dial in again and clicking the download link will pick up from where the last download left off. This turns an expensive, annoying catastrophe into no more than a minor irritation.

Virtual Gameboy

GAMES

http://www.komkon.org/fms/VGB/VGBWindows.html

It might seem a bit second-hand, but there is a way to play GameBoy games on your PC with this software.

Start-up tip

Change the registered owner – Bought a secondhand PC and it still displays the previous owner's name? A useful feature of regedit.exe is its ability to change the registered owner's name. Start, Run, type regedit, click OK and go to HKEY_LOCAL_MACHINE/Software/Microsoft/Windows/CurrentVersion. Highlight Current Version, click RegisteredOwner in the right hand pane, right-click, Modify and type in your new name.

VLMP   VIRTUAL MUSEUMS AND GALLERIES

http://www.comlab.ox.ac.uk/archive/other/museums

Not all museum sites have created a worthwhile virtual space to get absorbed in. The World Wide web Virtual Library museums pages by J. P. Bowen are a good place to start searches. Another good jumping-off point is **http://www.w3.org/hypertext/DataSources/bySubject/Overview2.html**. Look under Humanities for Museums. Also see **http://www.pacificrim.net/~mckenzie/jan96/museums.html**.